ABOUT THE AUTHORS

Colm O'Gorman is a lecturer in the Faculty of Commerce at University College Dublin, where he specialises in the areas of competitive strategy and enterprise development. He has published internationally in journals and books and presented papers on small business at international and national conferences. His research seeks to understand the development of competitive strategies in Irish SMEs. Specifically of interest are business level strategies associated with high growth. His Ph.D. thesis compared the strategic attributes and growth processes of high and low growth indigenous Irish companies.

James Cunningham is a lecturer in the Faculty of Commerce at the National University of Ireland, Galway. His main area of specialism is strategic management. His research interests include the impact of information technology on small businesses and structural change in emerging industries. His Ph.D. thesis focused on the impact of voluntary agreements on the competitive dynamics in Irish industry. Prior to joining the National University of Ireland, Galway, he lectured in the Faculty of Commerce at University College Dublin. He has completed a number of research projects in a variety of industry sectors. He has published internationally in journals and books and presented papers on strategic metaphors, strategy and the environment and the role of the strategist in post-modern organisations.

Irish Studies in Management

Editors:

W.K. Roche
Graduate School of Business
University College Dublin

Brian O'Kane
Oak Tree Press

Irish Studies in Management is a new series of texts and research-based monographs covering management and business studies. Published by Oak Tree Press in association with the Graduate School of Business at University College Dublin, the series aims to publish significant contributions to the study of management and business in Ireland, especially where they address issues of major relevance to Irish management in the context of international developments, particularly within the European Union. Mindful that most texts and studies in current use in Irish business education take little direct account of Irish or European conditions, the series seeks to make available to the specialist and general reader works of high quality which comprehend issues and concerns arising from the practice of management and business in Ireland. The series aims to cover subjects ranging from accountancy to marketing, industrial relations/ human resource management, international business, business ethics and economics. Studies of public policy and public affairs of relevance to business and economic life will also be published in the series.

ENTERPRISE IN ACTION

An Introduction to Entrepreneurship in an Irish context

Colm O'Gorman
James Cunningham

in association with
Graduate School of Business
University College Dublin

OAK TREE PRESS
19 Rutland Street
Cork, Ireland

© 2002 Individual contributors and the Michael Smurfit
Graduate School of Business, University College Dublin

A catalogue record of this book is
available from the British Library.

ISBN 1-86076-254-9

Printed in Ireland by Colour Books Ltd.

CONTENTS

FIGURES

CHAPTER 11
Encouraging and Supporting Entrepreneurship

CHAPTER 12
Community Enterprise

ACKNOWLEDGEMENTS

The authors wish to thank Sheila Flanagan (DIT) for contributing the chapter on Public Policy Enterprise Initiatives (Chapter 11) and Paul O'Reilly (DIT) for contributing the chapter on Networks and Alliances (Chapter 9).

The authors also wish to acknowledge the contribution of both post-graduate and undergraduate students of the Faculty of Commerce, University College Dublin and the National University of Ireland, Galway. Their theses and project work provided the inspiration for some of the chapters. Specifically, our thanks and recognition go to Kevin Dowdall, Joseph Gannon, Geraldine Lavin, Michael Madden, Geraldine O'Loughlin, and Aideen O'Toole. Finally the authors would like to thank Brian O'Kane and the staff of Oak Tree Press for their advice and assistance in developing this edition of the book.

This book is dedicated to

Clare

Sammi

FOREWORD

As both a practitioner and an academic, I have always found it difficult to get across to people the level of satisfaction, the buzz, of setting up your own business. Taking an idea, a concept or a vision or
what many will see as a hare-brained scheme, and turning it into an
operating reality is one of life's pleasures. Even the bad times are
good and, believe me, there will be bad times. The fact that the reality
often bears little resemblance to the initial idea matters not at all.

The heavy levels of work, worry and strain are all part of the
package, as are the mistakes that you will make. But you learn,
adapt, change, and keep moving forward. Financial success when it
comes, frequently with popular acclaim, is only the icing on the cake.
By then, you have done it, you have proven your beliefs to your own
satisfaction. That is my understanding of entrepreneurship. It is individuals with a vision willing to take risks to turn the vision into a
reality, with the ability to raise the resources necessary by whatever
means and the determination and energy to drive the project forward.
It is not a career for the many but, for the lucky few with the necessary characteristics, there is a world of opportunity waiting.

How vital are entrepreneurs in society? Critically important. A
vibrant, growing economy provides benefits and opportunities for
most, if not all, of its people. The vital element in the long-term success of an economy is a group of entrepreneurs creating the industries
of the future. These individuals look to the future, dream up opportunities and then, most importantly, make the dreams come true. Often, they fail, but that's how it should be.

For years it was believed, and it was more or les true, that the
Irish were not enterprising. Our culture and society directed people
into safe professions. The entrepreneurs emigrated. Business was not
a quality career. Attitudes have changed. For those of you with entrepreneurial tendencies, this means that you may now use those
scarce abilities in business rather than in some other area.

I am delighted to see the publication of this book. Entrepreneurship in Ireland has long been neglected by academics. The authors
not only examine current thinking and research into entrepreneur-

ship but also provide many pen-pictures of Irish entrepreneurs and their ventures. This gives a familiar, comfortable feel to the text.

The book is easy to read. For those of you who already know that you want to run your own business, *Enterprise in Action* will be a valuable companion. For those of you who wonder if you have "the calling", read the book. It could be the best few hours you will ever spend.

John J Teeling
Founder
Cooley Distillery plc, African Gold plc.

1

Profiling Irish Entrepreneurs[1]

Introduction

Do the likes of Dermot Desmond, Moya Doherty, Sean Melly, Fran Rooney, Lorraine Sweeney, Noel C. Duggan, Freda Hayes, Pat McDonagh, Padraig O'Ceidigh, Gene Browne and Albert Reynolds have unique advantages that equipped them to succeed as entrepreneurs? Why did these individuals choose to start their own business? What do we mean when we describe these individuals as entrepreneurs? Researchers, investors, bankers and potential entrepreneurs have always been interested in identifying what it takes to be a successful entrepreneur. This chapter will explore a number of different studies that have sought to identify a "success formula" for entrepreneurs. Reaching a conclusive answer to these questions is difficult. The research evidence suggests that there are some personality traits and background characteristics that are common to entrepreneurs but clearly there is no such thing as the typical entrepreneur.

The number and the profile of entrepreneurs in Ireland have changed significantly in recent years. The change has been more pronounced due the rapid growth of the Irish economy in the late 1990s. A number of important trends can be identified. The first trend is the role that small business has played in job creation in the US and in Europe during the 1980s and 1990s. In both the US and Europe large companies have been reducing their "headcount" by investing in technology and reorganising their businesses. While large companies have been reducing their levels of employment, the small business sector has been creating jobs. In Europe, where unemployment has remained high, small businesses have been slower to develop. The Irish government has begun to recognise the role that entrepreneurs play in wealth creation and job creation.

---

[1] The authors acknowledge the contribution of Michael Madden, a Masters of Business Studies Student at The Michael Smurfit Graduate School of Business. His thesis is "Characteristics and Motives of Entrepreneurs: An Enquiry into the Irish Food Sector" (1996).

Figure 1.1: "The Customer is King": Fergal Quinn and Superquinn

> *Fergal Quinn grew up in an environment that encouraged the idea of self-employment. His father was involved in a number of businesses, some of which were in the retail sector.*
>
> *In 1960 Fergal Quinn witnessed the changes that were beginning in European retailing. In particular the concept of self-service super-markets was emerging. He realised that these changes represented an opportunity and was determined that he would be among the leaders in retailing in Ireland. He opened his first store in late 1960 in Dun-dalk. From the beginning, he decided to specialise in fresh food and that he would be the best at everything he undertook.*
>
> *The company has grown significantly since 1960. It now has in ex-cess of 20% of the Dublin market and has stores in Kilkenny, Clonmel and Carlow. Fergal Quinn has continued to innovate throughout the development of Superquinn. He was the first supermarket to have in-store food manufacturing of products such as bread and sausages. Probably most important to Superquinn's success was that Fergal Quinn built an organisation that has remained close to the customer. Fergal Quinn believes that customers want high levels of service and that they like to interact with people and not machines.*
>
> *Fergal Quinn has "three big secrets of listening" to customers. The first secret is to tune into several different channels, for example Fer-gal Quinn has customer panels, customer service desks, formal market research. The second secret is that top management must listen to cus-tomers. To encourage this top managers in Superquinn have small of-fices, which ensures that they spend more time on the shop floor. The third secret is that listening must be focused on what the organisation wants to achieve. Fergal Quinn's philosophy is that "you must hear criticism if you want to improve customer service".[2]*

The second important trend is the increasing importance of the ser-vice sector. The service sector includes activities such as education, software, tourism, financial services, etc. In many service industries,, there are opportunities for small companies and self-employment.

The third trend is the changing job market. Organisations are re-designing themselves to be more competitive and flexible. This has resulted in out sourcing, short-term contracts, and flexible work prac-

[2] For further information on Fergal Quinn's management philosophy read his book *Crowning the Customer*.

tices. As the job market becomes less secure, individuals are more inclined to consider self-employment as a career choice.

The fourth significant trend is the emergence of female entrepreneurship. International research on entrepreneurs has traditionally focused on males. It has been assumed that entrepreneurs are male, and it has even been suggested that entrepreneurship is a way of demonstrating "maleness". However, the number of women operating their own business ventures has increased dramatically over the last decade. In the United States, one-quarter of small businesses are female-owned. Recent evidence suggests that women are now starting enterprises at two to five times the rate of men. Some forecasts suggest that close to 50% of all businesses will soon be run by women.

The first part of this chapter examines Irish entrepreneurs. This is followed by a discussion of international research evidence on entrepreneurs, first in terms of background characteristics and then in terms of personality traits. The role of the entrepreneur is considered and entrepreneurs are contrasted with managers. The chapter concludes with a discussion of different ways of studying entrepreneurs.

RESEARCH EVIDENCE ON IRISH ENTREPRENEURS

The Secrets of Success: Common Traits of Ireland's Leading Entrepreneurs

Research carried out at the Michael Smurfit Graduate School of Business profiled a number of leading Irish entrepreneurs.[3] These successful entrepreneurs were asked a basic question: *"To what do you contribute your success?"*. The focus of this research was on the individual entrepreneur rather than on the businesses they created. The answers received from this diverse group suggest that there are some common factors associated with entrepreneurial success. The common traits that emerged were:

- **Self-belief, Passion and Vision.** They had the ability to make their own decisions and to ignore what others were telling them, even so-called experts. According to the entrepreneurs, "to be an entrepreneur you must have an unshakeable belief in your ability, which means you never actually sit down and doubt yourself or your ability to do business". Self-belief is particularly important if you fail, as one entrepreneur commented: "if you are an

---

[3] Unpublished research work by students of the Diploma in Entrepreneurial Studies, supervised by Dr. C. O'Gorman.

entrepreneur in this country you'll get stoned, whereas if you're in
India, France, Germany or America they'll throw flowers at you".
All of the entrepreneurs were passionate about their business.
They all had some vision, dream or goal about their future. For
some, these images of the future emerged as they opportunistically
identified a new business. For many, starting up a business was
not work but rather an opportunity to do something that they
enjoyed.

- **Risk-Taking**. The entrepreneurs differed in terms of their
attitude to risk, some describing themselves as moderately
calculated risk-takers while others had to risk everything. The
greater the risk, the greater the buzz. However, they all believed
that the essence of entrepreneurship was about taking a risk.
What they have in common is that they took the risk and these
entrepreneurs saw opportunity where others saw risks.

- **Persistence and Hard work**. What drove Freda Hayes to set-up
House of James after leaving Blarney Woollen Mills and then
Meadows & Byrne? For her, starting up a business meant starting
at the bottom again. These successful entrepreneurs invested their
personal time into their businesses. Aristotle said that "we are
what we repeatedly do, excellence then is not an action but a
habit". Success rarely came quickly or easily. These individuals
refuse to give-up or to be set back by the failures that many of
them experienced. Denis O'Brien's initial venture, a shopping
channel on Sky television, failed, yet he has proved that he "has
the ability to pick himself up and run again". Some believed that
this ability is the defining characteristic of an entrepreneur.

- **Commitment to People ("Leadership")**. Many described an
essential quality of entrepreneurship as an ability to win the trust
of others, be they employees, customers or suppliers. However,
these entrepreneurs had little time for sentimentality: "if people
are not contributing to the organisation, get rid of them".

At one level, the entrepreneurs studied appeared to have little in
common. However, the differences identified tell an important story.
First, it was clearly evident that success was not restricted to any one
business sector. For many of the entrepreneurs, the choice of business
sector was purely opportunistic. Successful entrepreneurs are not just
found in emerging, changing high-growth sectors such as computer
software or telecommunications. Success was achieved in such di-

verse product and service areas as fast food, retailing, mineral water, manufacturing and stockbroking.

Prior experience in the field of entrepreneurial endeavour does not appear to be a pre-requisite for success. How did his job as a school-teacher prepare Pat McDonagh for his Supermac's venture? Conventional wisdom dictates that an entrepreneur should gain experience in the area before embarking on a new venture. Many entrepreneurs stumble into a particular area of activity that they have never worked in previously. For the entrepreneurs studied, it was never too early nor too late to embark on an entrepreneurial career. Many of the entrepreneurs had pursued structured career paths in traditional jobs, only later in life feeling that they were ready to take responsibility for creating their own wealth.

The qualities outlined above are common to the successful entrepreneurs studied. Taken together, they describe individuals from all walks of life who have identified an opportunity and have pursued it with a degree of single-mindedness that to an outsider may appear obsessive, unbalanced and unhealthy. It is clear that there is no success formula. Success in business, and success in any other area of endeavour such as sports, the arts, politics, comes to those who both seek it and preserve in the pursuit of it: "An entrepreneur looks for opportunity and seizes it".

Common Background Characteristics of Ireland's Leading Entrepreneurs

Studies of Irish entrepreneurs have tended to explore the background characteristics of the entrepreneur. These studies suggest that there are commonalities.

Education

Research on Irish entrepreneurs suggests that the level of educational attainment is high. Education appears to be correlated with high growth and the creation of ventures producing higher value-added products. A study by O'Farrell (1986) showed that 22% of manufacturing entrepreneurs had a degree at a time when only 9% of males in high population density areas had degrees. Education is more often in the areas of engineering, science and other technical disciplines rather than in commerce and business studies.

Previous Work Experience

Kinsella & Mulvenna (1993) found that over 75% of all individuals who set up their own firms held managerial positions in their employment immediately prior to "going it alone". Overseas experience is an important determinant of new business success in Ireland. Individuals who have experience of working abroad have a far greater propensity to export once they start their own firms. Also they make better use of contacts within the industry. O'Farrell showed that 42% of founders had worked abroad at some time in their career.

Parents' Occupation

Having self-employed parents increases the propensity of individuals to engage in new venture creation. O'Farrell's (1986) study showed that 46% of new firm founders had fathers who were self-employed at a time when only 27% of the population was self-employed.

Age at Start-up

Irish entrepreneurs are aged between 30 and 40 years at the time of new venture creation. The age of start-up in Ireland is less than that of UK entrepreneurs. This may be due to the wide availability of State grants and assistance in Ireland for some categories of entrepreneurship. Grants provide the entrepreneur with the seed capital required for start-up, removing the need for entrepreneurs to accumulate their own seed capital. Fast growth ventures are operated by entrepreneurs in the 35–44 age group,, whereas slower growing companies in the same industry are operated by founders mostly in the 45–54 age category.

Overall, the typical Irish entrepreneur is little different to entrepreneurs from other countries. The research evidence to date suggests that, relative to the average person, Irish entrepreneurs are educated to a higher level, often to degree level, and are more likely to be the eldest member of a family whose parents are self-employed. Relative to UK entrepreneurs, Irish entrepreneurs are younger at start-up. Irish entrepreneurs have progressed in their careers, often achieving managerial responsibilities. Overseas work experience is not unusual.

O'Farrell's research on Irish entrepreneurs in the manufacturing sector is summarised in Figure 1.1. These findings were in many ways mirrored by a study conducted in Northern Ireland by Hisrich (1988). Hisrich concluded that the predominant entrepreneur in the

North is independent, energetic, competitive, self-confident, and goal-oriented. Other characteristics identified are outlined in Figure 1.2.

Figure 1.2: Background Characteristics: An Historic Perspective – The O'Farrell Study

- Median age at time of establishment was 32.
- Majority of founders (84%) were under the age of 41.
- 84% were married.
- 73% held at least two full-time jobs prior to start-up.
- 22% held university degrees.
- 46% came from households where the father was self-employed.
- More than half of the sample of entrepreneurs had occupied managerial positions in their last job.
- 42% had engaged in full-time employment outside Ireland at some juncture in their career.
- Half of all new firms were established as partnerships.
- 27% of entrepreneurs were self-employed immediately prior to founding their present venture.

Figure 1.3: Hisrich Study: Characteristics of Entrepreneurs

- 40 years of age.
- Married with two children.
- 25% had degrees, mostly in business and engineering.
- Over one-half had previous experience in the business area.
- 50% had some form of managerial experience.
- Manufacturing firms were the most common.

The Motives for Start-up

Why do Irish people choose to be entrepreneurs? O'Farrell's (1986) study of Irish entrepreneurs identified a number of major motivational factors for starting a business:

- **Desire for independence**. One-third ranked this as their primary reason for start-up. Over 70% identified it as being in the top three reasons for starting a business.

- **Opportunity to exploit a gap in the market.** Thirty% ranked this as their primary reason for starting up.
- **Frustration.** This motive refers to individuals who felt blocked in their current jobs. They believed their autonomy and social mobility was impeded by the bureaucratic organisation they worked in. One-third of the respondents said "frustration" was one of the three most important factors in deciding to start-up a business.
- **Money.** To many, this may be surprising but only 10% ranked money as the number one motive for start-up. About one-third of respondents specified it as the second or third most important motive for start-up.
- Other less important reasons were redundancy, meeting a suitable business partner and a desire to return to work in Ireland.

These motives for starting a business can be classified either as "push" factors or "pull" factors. Motives classified as "push" are mainly negative in nature and include unemployment, frustration in a previous job, redundancy, and lack of promotional opportunities. Motives classified as "pull" include identifying a market opportunity, desire for independence, meeting a suitable business partner. Often an employee believed that the level of service or quality provided by their employer's business could be improved and decided to leave the business and start-up in competition.

INTERNATIONAL RESEARCH ON ENTREPRENEURS

The Background Characteristics of Entrepreneurs
Do entrepreneurs have common background characteristics? Do the background characteristics of entrepreneurs influence the likelihood of new venture creation? Do these characteristics influence the growth rate of the new business? The research evidence discussed above on Irish entrepreneurs suggests that there may be some characteristics common to all entrepreneurs. International research has suggested that entrepreneurs do share some common characteristics and that these are important in determining if an individual will consider becoming an entrepreneur.

Figure 1.4: Enterprising in Financial Services: Dermot Desmond[4]

Dermot Desmond has been involved in many ventures, most of which have a financial flavour. He believes that his success as an entrepreneur can be attributed to his ability to look at things in a different light. He says he never accepts the common wisdom or what everybody else says to be the case without first checking it out for himself. His advice to would-be entrepreneurs is to keep your eyes open at all times, be very patient and do not get frustrated no matter how long it takes. Some of his successes and business interests are:

- *In 1981 he founded National City Brokers (NCB), which became Ireland's largest independent stockbrokers. In 1994, he sold his 56% stake in NCB to Ulster Bank.*

- *He has a number of software businesses in Dublin, together with a number of financial businesses in Ireland and Europe. In 1984, he founded Quay Financial Software (QFS). Today QFS is a leading producer of digital platforms for dealing rooms. In July 1995, he sold his 80% share holding in QFS.*

- *He has a 50% stake in Pembroke Capital, an aviation leasing specialist. This company is staffed mainly by ex- Guinness Peat Aviation employees and concentrates on tax efficient international trading of aircraft.*

- *He purchased London City Airport in 1995. He plans to develop this into London's business airport for people with a preference for convenience and comfort.*

- *He pioneered the development of the International Financial Services Centre in Dublin.*

- *He has a significant holding in Celtic Football Club.*

- *He assisted Fran Rooney's purchase of Baltimore Technologies.*

Researchers have identified five background characteristics that have an important impact on entrepreneurs. While considering the research evidence presented below, it is important that three factors are borne in mind:

---

[4] The authors acknowledge and thank Darren Walsh, a graduate of the Diploma in Entrepreneurial Studies Programme, for his help in writing this piece.

- That the characteristics are not important in themselves but rather what is important is how the characteristics affect the behaviour of an individual.

- A person does not have to have these characteristics to become an entrepreneur.

- These characteristics are strongly associated and interrelated.

Level and Type of Education

Popular literature on entrepreneurship suggests that the entrepreneur attends the "university of hard knocks", that is, they learn about business by doing it rather than in school and university. This literature also suggests that entrepreneurs develop their managerial and technical expertise from their broad work experiences. Early research literature suggested that the level of education attained by entrepreneurs was lower than that of business executives, creating the myth of the "uneducated" entrepreneur. However, while the absolute level of educational attainment of entrepreneurs was low, there was evidence in this early research that the entrepreneurs had a higher level of educational attainment than the population as a whole. Recent research has demonstrated a clear link between level of educational attainment and propensity for entrepreneurial behaviour:

- Research studies of high technology ventures established a link between entrepreneurial success and level of education attained by the entrepreneur. However, performance at any given level of education does not appear to correlate with entrepreneurial behaviour.

- A review of 17 studies linking education and subsequent performance suggested that for 10 of them, a positive relationship was found, for six of them the results were not decisive and, in the remaining one, there was a negative relationship between education and performance (Cooper & Gascon, 1992). This suggests that a higher level of educational attainment may influence the probability of new venture creation, but it is difficult to isolate education as the independent factor responsible solely for business success.

- The relationship between new venture performance and the education of the entrepreneur may be dependent on the business sector the entrepreneur chooses. In some sectors, education may be the primary route to self-employment while, in other sectors, the opposite is the case. A college education is the primary route to self-employment in skilled services but, in the construction sector, the opposite situation prevails: high school drop-outs are much more likely to enter self- employment than college graduates. A study of high technology venture founders concluded that education does lead to substantially better performance.

- Attendance at college may be more important than the field of study. Attendance at college is important because it is seen as a broadening experience that involves the development of personal skills that would be helpful if a new venture is initiated. The experience of independence and the exposure to new ideas and people may motivate college graduates to start-up a new enterprise. College may be a surrogate for the development of other skills, such as communication skills and time management skills, which are useful to the entrepreneur.

Overall, the research evidence suggests that, in some sectors, the experience of education transfers certain skills and desires to participants. This may increase the propensity for new venture creation. Subsequent performance may also be related to the level of educational attainment, however performance at any given level of education does not affect propensity for new venture creation or subsequent new venture activity.

Previous Work Experience

The previous work experience of the entrepreneur influences the nature and success of the new business venture. Work experience may influence the choice of business sector and the size of the business created. The success of the new venture may be related to breadth of experience, to functional experience, and to the highest level of management experience of the entrepreneur. Prior experience in the business sector of the new venture activity is positively related to both new venture survival and growth. Familiarity with the sector allows the founder to make use of product and market knowledge and contacts.

The entrepreneur's involvement in previous ventures and the extent of the management role the entrepreneur had in such ventures are important determinants of success. Some authors have argued that the more times an entrepreneur has failed, the more likely they will be successful in the future. Entrepreneurs with higher levels of management experience tend to start-up larger enterprises. Entrepreneurs are frequently successful in their previous jobs. Overall, it appears that a majority of entrepreneurs initiate ventures that are

closely related to previous work experiences. Experience increases
the likelihood of being profitable, but experience plus education is
associated with the greatest success.

Parents' Occupation

Entrepreneurs are more likely to come from families in which their
parents owned a business. A household in which one or both parents
are self-employed will have exposed the potential founder to certain
skills, values and attitudes that will most likely aid them in the business world. Consequently, within the household, there will have been
a strong commitment to the ideology of a reward system inherent in
self-employment. The potential entrepreneur views their parents as
role models, and being "one's own boss" is perceived as a feasible career. This appears to be regardless of whether the parents were successful or unsuccessful. Over 50% of company founders in the United
States have self-employed fathers while only 12% of the work force
are self-employed.

Age at Start-up

Attempts to establish a link between the entrepreneur's age and the
performance of the new business have been inconclusive. The age of the
entrepreneur at start-up determines the experience of the entrepreneur
and may reflect the level of capital saved by the entrepreneur. There is
an argument that younger entrepreneurs are more likely to try and
grow their business. In trying to establish this link between the age
profile of the entrepreneur and the success of the business, it is important to remember that some sectors require a more experienced individual. Age alone may not be a predictor of new venture success, but
age may be a measure of experience and wealth accumulation, and
therefore a form of milestone that can trigger an individual towards
self-employment.

Birth Order of the Entrepreneur

Many studies have suggested that children who are the first-born in a
family are more likely to pursue an entrepreneurial career. The reason suggested for this is that the individual is subject to added attention and encouragement from their parents, resulting in the child developing more self-confidence. In a national sample involving over
400 female entrepreneurs, Hisrich & Brush (1984) found that 50%
were first-born.

Figure 1.5: Denis O'Brien: A "Classic" Success Story?

The launch of Esat Digifone in 1997 was a significant milestone for Denis O' Brien. Esat Digifone was Eircell's first competitor in the cellular mobile communications market in Ireland. Prior to launching Esat Digifone, Denis O'Brien had succeeded and failed in various businesses.

Denis was an Arts student in UCD and completed an MBA in Boston College, USA. During his student days, he was involved in a number of businesses that generated cash for himself. On completing his MBA, he got a job with a bank in Dublin with the intention of learning how banks work. He was determined at this stage that he would start-up his own business. A year later he left the bank and worked as a Personal Assistant to Tony Ryan of GPA. Denis worked hard with Tony Ryan and gained a lot of business experience. During this time, he learnt a number of important lessons:

"Don't invest money without putting in place good top management".

"If you go off-piste with investments you will go bankrupt — don't over-diversify your investments".

"Euphoria clouds an entrepreneur's judgement".

O'Brien left Tony Ryan and began a business called E-Sat TV. This company was to launch a shopping channel in the UK. It had a number of investors, including the Grattan Group plc, and over half a million pounds invested. The venture was in trouble from the beginning. Sales did not materialise. He responded quickly by rationalising. Staff were let go and the programme was redesigned. However, due to their own financial difficulties, the Grattan Group had to "pull the plug" on the venture. E-Sat TV closed and O'Brien wound up the venture.

At the time, the Irish government was advertising for licences for the new private broadcasting sector. He successfully obtained a licence. He hired Australians to run the business because the Australian radio market is very competitive. He organised a very high profile launch for his station Classic Hits 98FM. The radio station has continued to invest in market research to ensure that they deliver what customers want. Since then, he has opened radio stations in Prague, Stockholm and Vilnius.

The next business that Denis turned his attention to was the telecommunications business. He founded Esat Telecom and applied for a licence to lease lines from Telecom Eireann (now eircom). He wanted

> *to sell cheaper calls to corporate customers. After a year of problems and complaints to the Competition Directorate of the EU, he got the licence. One of his biggest ventures was the winning of the second mobile phone licence in Ireland. This was against strong international competition. He subsequently sold Esat to British Telecom, which rebranded the telecoms group Esat BT, while the mobile phone division was rebranded O2. Shortly after BT's purchase of the Esat Group, the value of BT's stock was hot be the general downturn in telecoms stocks. This meant that BT, under the stewardship of Bill Murphy, had to bring Esat BT into profit by 2002 to avoid being divested.*

Psychological Characteristics of Entrepreneurs

It is more likely that entrepreneurs will have common personality traits than common background characteristics. Most people will identify entrepreneurs as risk-takers and as having a strong determination to succeed. It is difficult to measure personality traits as researchers can never be sure of the measurement or the significance of a personality trait. The most popular personality traits examined in the literature on entrepreneurs are need for achievement, risk-taking propensity, internal/external locus of control, need for independence and type-A behaviour syndrome.

Need for Achievement

A high need for achievement (nAch) has been accepted as a principle motivator of entrepreneurial behaviour since the early 1960s. Entrepreneurs with this trait value excellence, they stay focused and committed to a task, and this burning desire to be a winner sustains their involvement even in uncertain times. McClelland (1961) described the characteristics of high need achievement, which are illustrated in Table 1.3.

Interestingly, entrepreneurs with a high need for achievement view profits as a measure of success, and money as a feedback mechanism not a goal in itself. These individuals will remain optimistic even in the most unfamiliar of situations. In choosing advisors, high need achievers will select experts rather than family and friends to help them. Other findings associated with high nAch entrepreneurs is that they are more energetic, persistent, realistic and more action-minded than individuals who display other kinds of motivational patterns.

Figure 1.6: McClelland's Characteristics of High Need Achievement

- Preference for decisions involving risk that are neither very high risk or very low risk.
- Belief that one's efforts will be influential in the attainment of some goal.
- Perceive the probability of success in attaining a goal as being relatively high.
- Need for feedback.
- Capacity to plan ahead.
- Desire to take personal responsibility for decisions.
- An interest in excellence for its own sake.
- Interest in concrete results from decisions.

Locus of Control

The locus of control scale developed by Rotter (1966) measures a person's perceived ability to influence events in their lives. Individuals with an internal locus of control believe that their own behaviour determines their destiny, and give little credence to "external" forces such as destiny, luck or "powerful others". Individuals with an external locus of control don't believe in their ability to control their external environment and are reluctant to assume the risks that starting a business would entail.

Studies suggest that locus of control is useful for distinguishing entrepreneurs from the general population, but it is not a valid discriminator of entrepreneurs and managers. Managers and entrepreneurs were both characterised as internals. Rotter (1966) argued that an internal control locus of control was consistent with a high achievement orientation. Individuals who portray internal values and beliefs are more likely to have a higher need for achievement.

Risk-Taking Propensity

Much research has been carried out examining the risk-taking propensity of entrepreneurs compared to managers. This research is plagued by measurement problems. It is appropriate to characterise entrepreneurs as moderate to high risk-takers, especially at the outset, but, as the business evolves and grows, these same individuals display calculated tendencies towards risk, preferring to take gambles they feel are within their own ability to control. Entrepreneurs can be characterised as opportunity-seekers rather than risk-takers. It seems that the biggest risk an entrepreneur takes is deciding to leave a job in order to start a new venture. Many studies have found that an entrepreneur's tendency to take risks actually reduces as the firm's net worth increases. This is because entrepreneurs have a substantial asset base to protect. By taking over an existing business rather than starting a new business, the entrepreneur can reduce the element of risk involved.

Tolerance for Ambiguity

Tolerance for ambiguity can be defined as the tendency to perceive ambiguous situations as desirable rather than threatening. Entrepreneurs are viewed as people capable of sustaining the drive and determination to persist with a course of action even when future outcomes are uncertain. It is this willingness to tolerate uncertainty that separates entrepreneurs from "would-be entrepreneurs". This element complements the risk-taking facet previously examined and both are used by researchers in studying potential entrepreneurial subjects. Persons with a high tolerance for ambiguity and a moderate to high risk-taking propensity are the ones most likely to succeed despite, or indeed in spite of, all obstacles that are in their way. They are motivated by a challenge and regard simplicity as uneventful.

Type A Behaviour

People can be classified into two different types of behaviours. Type A people are involved in an aggressive struggle to achieve more and more in less and less time, which manifests itself in such tendencies as impatience, time urgency, driving ambition, and competitiveness. Type B individuals are characterised as more easy-going and as less competitive in relation to daily events. Entrepreneurs were found to exhibit a majority of the Type A elements, particularly in relation to the hurried and impatient variables. In some instances, they also can become over-obsessive, which can hinder their capacity to perform efficiently.

Need for Independence

Entrepreneurs are typically characterised as people who prefer to do things on their own, in their own way, and also in their own time. This need mostly stems from a feeling of being blocked and contained in past bureaucratic organisations. Many individuals just can't relate to or adapt to order-taking in an employer/   employee relationship. They seek out situations where they can have complete control and personal impact on the results. Research suggests that "being independent" is the major significant factor for entrepreneurs being glad for having started a business.

Figure 1.7: David McKenna – From Plumbing to Recruitment

> *David left school at 15 and served his time as a plumber in London. In 1993, he set up a recruitment agency with €7,618 of capital to invest. This was before the real boom in the Irish economy. By 1997, the company has in excess of 80,000 CVs on file and the future looked bright. This led to the listing of Marlborough International on the Stock Exchange, which netted David in excess of €5 million cash as well as a paper valuation of €12.70 million. He became CEO of the newly-listed company. Subsequently, the company came under financial pressure due to the consolidation in the recruitment market. Due to this and other factors, Marlborough International was delisted, broken up and sold to interested parties during the first few months of the new century.*

WHAT IS THE ROLE OF THE ENTREPRENEUR?

Defining the Entrepreneur

In this chapter, discussion has centred on the common background characteristics and the common personality traits of entrepreneurs. There are numerous definitions of entrepreneurs but it is difficult to identify exactly who is and who isn't an entrepreneur (Figure 1.8). Would you include the owner of a small business as an entrepreneur? Is Michael Smurfit an entrepreneur? Is an investor on the stock exchange an entrepreneur? Is , founder of the charity GOAL, an entrepreneur? Is your dentist, solicitor or GP an entrepreneur? Can you be an entrepreneur within an existing business? While an exact definition is difficult to reach, there appears to be factors common to many of these definitions. Figure 1.8 sets out what seem to be the essential elements of entrepreneurship.

Opportunity Recognition

Entrepreneurs must identify an opportunity if they are to start-up in business. The source of this idea might be previous work experience,

experience of purchasing or using a product/service, the purchase of a franchise, the development or invention of a product. However, identifying an opportunity is not enough, the entrepreneur must exploit this opportunity.

Uncertainty

Entrepreneurs must deal with market uncertainties. They cannot know the level of future demand for the product/service or whether they will be able to produce the product/service at the required cost. Also a significant uncertainty facing many entrepreneurs centres around obtaining the necessary finance for the venture. Typically entrepreneurs must commit their own financial resources without the full knowledge that others will invest in the project.

Risk-taking

The entrepreneur takes a business risk, a financial risk and a personal risk. The business risk is that the entrepreneur does not know whether their new business idea will be successful. There is uncertainty surrounding future demand for the product/service. Therefore, the entrepreneur must make a judgement as to the size of potential demand. The entrepreneur takes a financial risk by investing money in the new business. This begins with the investment of time and money in preparing a feasibility study and developing a prototype of the product. This is followed by investment in the purchase of equipment and/or the purchase of a lease for the business. If the business fails, the entrepreneur may be indebted to a bank and may have difficulty in getting business or personal credit in the future. The entrepreneur takes a significant personal risk when starting-up a new business. If the business fails, it may be difficult for the entrepreneur to get back into paid employment. In addition, failure is still regarded as a social taboo in this country.

Resource-gathering

The entrepreneur has to gather the resources needed for the business, which includes financial resources and others such as human, information and technical resources. The entrepreneur will rarely have all the resources needed in a start-up situation.

Figure 1.8: Definitions of Entrepreneurs

- The Irish-born French economist Cantillion is credited as being the first to use the term *entrepreneur*. He defined the entrepreneur as "the agent who purchases the means of production and combines them into marketable products".

- The entrepreneur is "the owner or manager of a business enterprise who, by risk and initiative, attempts to make profits" (Collins English Dictionary).

- Entrepreneurship: ". . . is the process of identifying opportunities in the marketplace, marshalling the resources to pursue these opportunities and committing the actions and resources necessary to exploit the opportunities for long-term personal gain" (Sexton & Bowman-Upton, 1991).

- The entrepreneur is a person who ". . . creates a venture and institutes practices intended to increase the firm's size" (Johnson, 1990).

- "Entrepreneurs are 'opportunistic decision makers' who identify and capitalise on opportunities through approaches that emphasise innovation, profitable venture identification, effectiveness, and non-programmed or ambiguous situations" (Olson, 1986).

- "The entrepreneur, by definition, shifts resources from areas of low productivity and yield to areas of higher productivity and yield. Of course, there is a risk the entrepreneur may not succeed" (Drucker, 1985).

- "Entrepreneurship is the ability to create and build a vision from practically nothing: fundamentally it is a human, creative act. It is the application of energy to initiating and building an enterprise or organisation, rather than just watching or analysing. This vision requires a willingness to take calculated risks — both personal and financial — and then to do everything possible to reduce the chances of failure. Entrepreneurship also includes the ability to build an entrepreneurial or venture team to complement your own skills or talent. It is the knack for sensing an opportunity where others see chaos, contradiction, and confusion. It is possessing the know-how to find, marshal, and control resources (often owned by others)" (Timmons, Smollen and Dingee, 1985).

Profits / Reward

The entrepreneur engages in the above activities for personal gain. The entrepreneur receives rewards in a number of ways. The first is reward as salary. This is the reward for the time the entrepreneur puts into the business. In most small businesses, the entrepreneur rewards himself with a low salary, preferring instead to keep the money in the business. The second is return on invested capital. The entrepreneur should receive a return for the money invested in the business. In a similar way as an investor expects a return on invested capital, the entrepreneur should expect to receive a return on the money invested in the business. This return may be in the form of a dividend or more typically in terms of a capital gain. The third is reward for taking the risk. The entrepreneur should receive a return for the risk taken. The capital gains of the initial investment should reflect the business risk of the investment.

Figure 1.9: Riches from Rags: The Story of Jai Morrissey of JMS

In 1992 Jai Morrissey, at the age of 26, started her own Irish fashion company. Hers was the only company in Ireland at the time to manufacture bespoke tailor-made shirts.

Jai Morrissey had always wanted to work in the fashion business. After four years studying Art & Design in Waterford and Limerick, she returned to her home town. She designed and made a dress for her sister's "debs" dance. This was so well received by people that she was asked to make more. This brought her to the attention of some Waterford businessmen. They asked her to supply them with sheepskin sleeveless jackets. However, this was a very labour-intensive process and Jai found it was impossible to be price competitive with cheaper Turkish imports. This business failed because Jai was unable to raise money from her own sources, from banks or from any State agencies.

Within a couple of weeks of this business failing, Jai got a job as trainee buyer at Penney's. Within two years, she had been promoted to assistant buyer. In this job, she learned about consumer requirements, computers and doing business with others. During her holidays, she applied for a job in Trinity Shirts as a handcutter. Trinity Shirts was the only bespoke (i.e. custom made) shirt manufacturer in Ireland. This job gave Jai an opportunity to get back into mainstream fashion. She was promoted quickly to manager in Trinity Shirts. However, Trinity Shirts was an old company and continued to offer only one classic style. This lead to financial difficulties, job losses and the closure of the company.

> *Jai Morrissey had a number of opportunities open to her. However, she chose to start up her own business. An important factor in making this decision was the inspiration she received from her father. He was self-employed, had worked hard, enjoyed his job and provided for his family. Being self-employed would allow her to do what she enjoyed most, designing clothes.*
>
> *Jai began to examine the business she knew best: bespoke shirt manufacturing. She was personally known to the buyers in this business and was able to establish that they would be interested in purchasing from her. Jai was aware that her previous employer had been unsuccessful in raising finance when it got into financial difficulties.*
>
> *Even though she was unsure how to write a business plan, she produced one. She sent this plan to ministers in different government departments. They all referred her back to the IDA. However, because her prospective employment was five, she did not meet the minimum requirement of 15 that the IDA had imposed for the clothing sector.*
>
> *After eight weeks of writing the plan and trying to raise finance, Jai was referred to the Finglas Partnership. The Partnership was enthusiastic about the business and put her in touch with the Business Innovation Centre. She secured premises and a low rate loan to purchase a sewing machine and in November of 1992 she started her own business.*

How is Entrepreneurship Different from Management?

The famous economist Joseph Schumpeter (1948) wrote extensively on entrepreneurship as a means of creating something new. He discounted all managers and heads of firms from his definition. His belief was that something innovative had to occur in order for a person or persons to call themselves an entrepreneur. This could include the introduction of a new product, a new method of production, the opening and entering of a new market, or the finding of a new source of raw material. To finance one or more of the above innovations, the entrepreneur must convince money holders of the worthiness of the innovation. This definition, especially if used in today's context, would lead us to the conclusion that only a small minority of business owners could rightly call themselves entrepreneurs. Most businesses are just clones of other similar operations.

The entrepreneur differs from the manager in their approach to opportunities and resources. The entrepreneur seeks new opportunities while the manager seeks to protect and build on the existing set of resources. Managers are charged with the stewardship of existing resources; they must protect the resources that a firm owns. The entrepreneur seeks to commit resources to opportunities quickly. They commit resources without knowing whether they will be able to acquire the other resources necessary to make the venture a success. In contrast, the manager will frequently commit resources only after carefully researching an opportunity.

DIFFERENT WAYS OF STUDYING ENTREPRENEURS

In this chapter, we have reviewed a number of studies of entrepreneurs and have sought to identify common traits and characteristics and to establish what exactly an entrepreneur does. There are a number of different ways of studying entrepreneurs. These can be classified into a number of "schools" of thought.

The "Background Characteristics" School

The study of entrepreneurship has traditionally emphasised the background characteristics of the entrepreneur. These studies explore variables such as education, age at start-up, birth order, and parents' occupation. Entrepreneurs are often contrasted with managers and executives in these studies. More recently, entrepreneurs have been compared with other entrepreneurs, for example high growth and low growth entrepreneurs, male and female entrepreneurs. The appeal of this approach is that it is easy to collect the data but this method is of limited benefit to individual entrepreneurs and public policy-makers.

The "Personality Traits" School

An alternative approach is to study the personality traits of entrepreneurs. The basis of this school of thought is that an individual's needs, attitudes, beliefs and values are the prime determinants of behaviour. This school believes that entrepreneurs have unique values and attitudes towards work and life, which cause them to act differently to others. Therefore, entrepreneurs can be differentiated according to characteristics such as risk-taking propensity, need for achievement, and locus of control.

The "Born to Entrepreneurship" School

Some authors believe that individuals are born with the skills and aptitudes necessary for success. Entrepreneurs are considered to be charismatic leaders, to be inspirational, with the ability to communicate ideas and concepts to other people in a way that is interesting, appealing or engaging. These authors believe that entrepreneurs have some sort of natural intuition that enables them to grasp opportunities. Popular literature adopts this perspective by portraying the entrepreneur as a hero and charismatic leader, for example Lee Iaccoca and Richard Branson.

The "Process" School

The process school's central tenet is that an entrepreneur is a person who organises or manages a business undertaking, assuming the risk for the sake of profit. It believes that entrepreneurship can be taught, and so it aims to identify the functions involved and provide training to existing and would-be entrepreneurs. The provision of training in management activities such as marketing and finance should, it is hoped, reduce the number of business failures. As is self-evident from this school of thought, it assumes that entrepreneurs can be "made", which is in direct contrast to the "born to entrepreneurship" school.

The "Intrapreneurship" School

Intrapreneurship involves the creation of independent business units designed to create, market, and expand innovative services, technologies, or methods within the organisation. This approach is appropriate to studying entrepreneurship in large organisations. In these organisations, some individuals are given freedom to act in an entrepreneurial way, without having to take on ownership responsibility. These individuals are referred to as corporate entrepreneurs or more commonly as "intrapreneurs".

The "Behavioural" School

Another approach to the study of entrepreneurs is to focus on the behaviours of the entrepreneurs. This school studies the management practices that are associated with successful entrepreneurship. Entrepreneurs are essentially people who make things happen. In this way, they can be classified by their behaviour in how they approach problems, how they delegate responsibilities, and so on. It is a person's behaviour that determines whether they are defined as an entrepreneur and therefore it is more appropriate to study entrepreneurial behaviour than background characteristics. It is behaviour, rather than personality, that will best improve our understanding of entrepreneurship. More recent studies have focused on the business that the entrepreneur creates rather than on the entrepreneur who creates the business. These researchers examine the market entry and competitive strategies of the new business.

Figure 1.10: Riverdance: Seven Minutes of a Space Filler

> *Moya Doherty producer of the European Song Contest in 1994 was the originator of the seven-minute space-filler, which included Gene Butler and Michael Flatley, that subsequently became" Riverdance". Riverdance, the Show has become world's largest stage show and one of Ireland's biggest exports. The merchandising, video, ticket and album sales have made its co-creator and producer, Doherty, who risked all in 1995, her partner John McColgan and composer Bill Whelan, into multi-millionaires. Moreover, Doherty and McColgan own Tyrone Productions, which produces programmes such as Who Wants to be a Millionaire and Ras na Rí for TG4. They had a minority share in Radio Ireland, the predecessor to Today FM.*

CONCLUSION

There are an ever-increasing number of entrepreneurs in Ireland and there is evidence that there are an increasing number of female entrepreneurs. This chapter identified the factors that contribute to the likelihood of an individual considering a "career" as an entrepreneur. It identified the common background characteristics of entrepreneurs and the common personality traits of entrepreneurs. There are a number of different ways to study an entrepreneur. Studying personality traits and background characteristics are only two of many ways to study an entrepreneur.

QUESTIONS

1. What are the background characteristics of Irish entrepreneurs? Why do entrepreneurs have these characteristics?

2. Identify the common personality traits of successful entrepreneurs.

3. What are the different ways of studying entrepreneurs? Which of these approaches do you consider to be the most useful?

4. In a group, identify the five entrepreneurs you most admire. Now identify the five words that best describe entrepreneurs. Do these "words" describe the entrepreneurs you identified?

5. Interview an entrepreneur in your locality to establish the reasons for their success. Use this interview to test the ideas presented in this chapter.

6. From sources in your library, write a short history of an entrepreneur that you admire.

REFERENCES

Cooper, A. & J. Gascon (1992): "Entrepreneurs, Processes of Founding, and New Firm Performance", in *State of the Art of Entrepreneurship Research*, Sexton, D. & J. Kasda, (eds.) Boston, MA: PWS-Kent.

Drucker, P.F. (1985): *Innovation and Entrepreneurship*, New York: Harper and Row.

Hisrich, R. & C. Brush (1988): "Women Entrepreneurs: Strategic Origins Impact on Growth" in *Frontiers of Entrepreneurship Research* (eds.) B. Kirchhoff, W. Long, W. McMullan, K. Vesper & W. Wetzel, Jr., Wellesley, MA: Babson College.

Hisrich, R. (1988): "The Entrepreneur in Northern Ireland: Characteristics, Problems, and Recommendations for the Future", *Journal of Small Business Management*, 26 (3), pp. 32–39.

Johnson, B.R. (1990): "Towards a Multidimensional Model of Entrepreneurship: The Case of Achievement Motivation and the Entrepreneur", *Entrepreneurship: Theory and Practice*, 14 (3), pp. 39–54.

Kinsella, R. & D. Mulvenna (1993): "Fast Growth Firms: Their Role in the Post-Culliton Industrial Strategy", *Administration*, 41 (1), pp. 3–15.

McClelland, D.C. (1961): *The Achieving Society*, Princeton, NJ: Van Nostrand.

Murray, A. (1983): "In Search of Entrepreneurship", *Journal of Irish Business and Administrative Research*, pp. 41–55.

O'Farrell, P. (1986): *Entrepreneurs and Industrial Change*, Dublin: IMI.

Olson, P.D. (1986): "Entrepreneurs: Opportunistic Decision Makers", *Journal of Small Business Management*, 24 (3), pp. 29–35.

Rotter, J.B. (1966): "Generalized Expectancies for Internal versus External Control of Reinforcement", *Psychological Monographs*, 80: No. 609.

Schumpeter, J.A. (1948): Economic Theory and Entrepreneurial History, Change and the Entrepreneur, Cambridge, MA: Harvard University.

Sexton, D.L. and Bowman-Upton, N. (1991): Entrepreneurship: Creativity and Growth, New York: Macmillan.

Timmons, J. (1994): New Venture Creation, Homewood, IL: Irwin.

2

START-UP STRATEGIES

INTRODUCTION

There are many different ways to start a new business. Richard Branson began his entrepreneurial career in the music business with no experience and few resources. However, his entry into the condom business, the cola business and the airline business were very different. In these businesses, he sought to become a significant competitor from the start. Though he continued to lack industry-specific experience, he had the resources to make large investments and to seek market share quickly.

There are many business opportunities and most start-ups never make it into the headlines. The start-ups that receive most popular attention tend to be either highly successful and innovative products, for example Tetra-Pak, or novelty products. The choice of how to become an entrepreneur will depend on the nature of the business opportunity that interests the entrepreneur and the resources and experiences of the entrepreneur. This chapter reviews the strategies that entrepreneurs pursue when starting a new business. It examines the start-up period and identifies problems that are common to many new businesses.

STARTING A NEW BUSINESS

There are several alternative routes to becoming an entrepreneur.

Copy an Existing Business Idea

This is by far the most common route into entrepreneurship. Most new businesses copy an existing business and apply it to a new geographic area. Most service-type businesses such as hairdressers, video shops, restaurants, builders and most professional businesses such as solicitors, opticians and electricians are examples of an entrepreneur copying an existing business idea. A more successful variant of this approach to new business start-up is to copy a business opportunity from an overseas market. Many new business ideas in Ireland originate from the US and the UK.

• The advantage of this approach is that the business has a proven product/service idea. Also it may be easy to identify potential customers, who are the people using the product/service of competitors. This is also a disadvantage in that it may be difficult to develop any competitive advantage and to persuade existing customers to change supplier. Competitors may be able to react quickly to any innovations that the new business introduces.

Figure 2.1: Aircoach — Challenging Dublin Bus

Aircoach started operating a bus route from Dublin Airport to city centre hotels in 1999, competing head-on with Dublin Bus. Dublin Bus reacted to this new service by improving the frequency of its services and the quality of its buses. Aircoach had considerable difficulty in getting its service established due to signage and other difficulties it experienced. It also launched a service from the airport to the Docklands, which was not a success because of business travellers' reluctance to take a bus. In 2001, the company carried approximately 60,000 passengers a month. In 2002, Aircoach turned the corner with its original airport/city centre route. Moreover, it also sought additional investors to fund four new routes from the airport to Leopardstown, Tallaght, Rathgar and Greystones and to run nine coaches on the Cork/Dublin route for an initial nine services a day in both directions.

Develop a New Product/Service

Most people consider that it is essential to do something new if they are to start a new business. However, this strategy has the highest risk and the highest failure rate. For every new idea that is commercially successful, there are a large number that fail. The advantages of developing a new product/service are that there may be an opportunity for rapid market penetration. Also, by being first into the market, the new business may get some "first mover" advantages. First-mover advantages may be the development of a brand image, acquiring the best locations and distribution outlets or patent protection, if the product is a technical innovation. However, being first to the market does not guarantee success. Many new ideas are copied by existing businesses that may have a brand image or better access to distribution outlets. Often the first-mover carries the cost of developing both the product and the market, allowing later entrants to pursue a lower cost strategy — "pioneers get arrows in their backs". In many industries, it is possible to be too innovative, too far ahead of what the market and customers are prepared to accept.

Figure 2.2: Anita Roddick sets up "The Body Shop"

> *In 1971, Anita Roddick, a teacher, and her husband established a small hotel and restaurant in Littlehampton in England. This was not fulfilling enough for the ambitious Anita and she started to look for another business opportunity. In 1976, she arrived at the idea of selling appropriately packaged naturally-based cosmetics. Anita had travelled extensively and knew of 12 natural ingredients that were used as cosmetics in other parts of the world. She obtained a bank loan of stg£6,000, developed a list of 25 products and contacted a manufacturing chemist in the area. She opened her new shop, The Body Shop, on Saturday 27 March, 1976.*

Figure 2.3: Patrick Campbell and the "Campbell Bewley Group"

> *Patrick Campbell was born into a catering family. His parents operated several bed & breakfast businesses and a hotel. Patrick Campbell studied hotel management at the College of Catering in Cathal Brugha Street, Dublin. He then worked in various hotels in Ireland, the UK and Sweden. On returning home, he worked in the family business. However, the business was only busy during the four-month tourist season and Patrick Campbell became frustrated. He wanted a bigger challenge. In 1967, he and his wife set-up a catering company, Campbell Catering, to supply catering services to outdoor events. At this time, there were very few providers of contract catering. This business was not very capital-intensive so they could start with very little money, however one of their first contracts, making sandwiches, nearly closed the business.*

Figure 2.4: The Hangover that led to the "Ballygowan" Brand

> *The germ of the "Ballygowan" brand was born when Geoff Read was working in London as a shoe salesman. Suffering from a hangover one day, he left the shop to buy a cure and he was struck by the fact that all the bottled water came from France. In 1979, he took a two-month AnCo course and undertook a feasibility study for this bottled water idea.*

> *The decline in the quality of tap water, more sophisticated consumers due to foreign travel and a retreat from alcohol due to health reasons convinced Read that there could be explosive growth for bottled water. The name "Ballygowan" originated from an adaptation of a local townland. He did a deal with a farmer to access a spring and, from his garage, he started to fill his bottles. His initial seed capital was €5,000. In order to grow the business, Read did a deal with Richard Nash in Newcastlewest, an independent bottler and manufacturer of drinks. The deal meant that Nash would do the production and Read the marketing, with Read having an option to buy back Nash's 50% share. Ballygowan's marketing was simple – product placement.*
>
> *In 1989, Perrier's reputation was decimated by a benzene contamination. This resulted in Britvic, the second biggest drinks distributor in Britain, dropping Perrier in favour of Ballygowan. This opportunity gave Ballygowan 250,000 new outlets. In 1993, Read sold Ballygowan to Cantrell and Cochrane.*

Buy/Franchise an Existing Business

There are a number of variants to this strategy. These include franchising a business, licensing a product from an inventor or company, and acquiring an existing business.

Franchising is where the entrepreneur purchases the right to operate a business. Examples of successful franchises are McDonalds, Abrakebabra and Supermac's. Franchising accounts for one-third of all US retail sales.

Licensing is different from franchising in that the entrepreneur buys the right to manufacture or distribute a product in a region. The entrepreneur pays the inventor or developer a royalty for every product sold. Inventors and businesses license their products because they may not have the skills, resources or time to develop the product in all markets. Licensing is very common in the computer software business among developers of computer games.

The advantage of these strategies is that the entrepreneur gets a proven business idea. In the case of a franchise, the entrepreneur gets a complete package that may include business training (Figure 2.5). However these strategies can be very expensive. Franchises require an up-front investment and an on-going payment of a percentage of sales revenues or profits to the franchisee (Figure 2.6). Also, growth opportunities for franchise holders may be limited.

Buying an existing business has the added advantage of giving the entrepreneur an established customer base.

Figure 2.5: Advantages and Disadvantages of Franchising

For the Franchiser (seller of the franchise):
- **Advantages**:   Rapid expansion of the business
  Increased income
  Less time spent operating the business
  Access to more capital.
- **Disadvantages**: Have to identify suitable franchisees
  Difficulty in keeping control.

For the Franchisee (buyer of the franchise):
- **Advantages**:   Business format tested and proven
  Often a recognised business name,
  therefore existing brand loyalty
  Advice available from franchiser and other
  Franchisees.
- **Disadvantages**: Initial up-front costs
  Fees increase as business grows
  Limited autonomy to change or improve the
  Business.

Figure 2.6: Financial Considerations for the Franchisee

- **Initial Franchisee Fee**: Usually 5 to 10% of start-up costs
- **Franchise Package**: The cost of fixture and fittings, initial stock, etc
- **Management Services Fee**: Ongoing costs for rights to the franchise. Average of 3 to 15% of turnover
- **Advertising Levy**: Contribution to central advertising fund. Usually 2.5 to 5% of gross turnover
- **Exclusive Purchase of Product**: May have to purchase goods from franchiser or nominated supplier.

THE NEW VENTURE CREATION PROCESS

The Start-up Period

How does an entrepreneur feel during the launch of a new business? The problems and experiences of entrepreneurs who have started their own business are surprisingly similar. Research into the process of starting a new business attempts to identify and categorise these common events.

Common emotions experienced by an entrepreneur at start-up are:

- **Relief**: The difficult decision to start-up the business has been made and attention is now directed at running the new business.

- **Stress**: The entrepreneur is under constant pressure.

- **Time Pressure**: Starting a business is very time-consuming. The entrepreneur is doing everything for the first time. Most entrepreneurs work day and night, seven days a week, during the early days of the business.

- **Uncertainty**: The entrepreneur does not know whether the business will succeed or fail.

- **"Out of Control"**: The entrepreneur is dependent on others for the success of the business. Customers, bankers, investors, staff and suppliers are all putting pressure on the entrepreneur to "deliver the goods".

- **Under-resourced**: The entrepreneur does not have the financial, managerial and personnel resources to cope with all the demands on the business.

- **Excitement**: The start-up period is an exhilarating period for most entrepreneurs. Usually there will be a sense of commitment and enthusiasm among employees with everybody trying to help get the business up and running.

Not all start-up businesses follow the same pattern.

Some start small and grow and develop very slowly. In some sectors, entrepreneurs might start working on their new business at week-ends. As demand for the business develops, the entrepreneur may consider leaving full-time employment and devoting all their time to the business. In many cases, these businesses may never be very profitable but the entrepreneur prefers to be self-employed rather than an employee.

Other businesses grow very quickly, because the entrepreneur has developed a successful product or service. Some businesses must grow quickly if they are to earn enough to repay the large amounts of capital invested.

These alternative start-up patterns are described below.

Figure 2.7: Chris Horn sets up "IONA Technologies"[5]

IONA Technologies was founded in March 1991 by three academics, Dr. Chris Horn, Annraí O'Toole and Dr. Sean Baker of the Computer Science Department at Trinity College, Dublin. Horn and his colleagues had been actively involved in the development of the CORBA (Common Object Request Broker Architecture) standard, established by a pan-computer industry movement in 1989 to set a standard for Object Technology Software before one main player dominated the market. They also worked on ESPRIT Research and Development projects from 1985 to 1991. This research work under ESPRIT exposed them to the emerging technologies in the software industry.

Chris Horn, Sean Baker and Annraí O'Toole set out to develop software to implement the CORBA standard. The trio established IONA as a campus company, which enabled them to exploit their research commercially while retaining their positions as university staff members. Although the number of staff directly involved in IONA was small, other academics and researchers were indirectly involved in the early stages, providing welcome support when necessary. The three spent one year writing the code for their product. IONA's mission was to bring the power of Distributed Object Technology to the world.

The development of IONA was funded from the founders' own resources, after attempts to raise outside finance received little interest from banks, venture capitalists or investors. Like many software companies, IONA Technologies had to become involved in consultancy and specialist computer training to fund the research and development of its software product. IONA developed specialist training packages for other providers of computer training. "In the early days, the profits from consultancy and training paid the wages of those who were developing Orbix", recalls Horn. The company has grown rapidly since launching its main product, Orbix, in 1993. The company went public on the New York NASDAQ market in 1997.

[5] Profile written by Dr. C. O'Gorman and Geraldine Lavin.

"Bootstrapping"

"Bootstrapping" describes start-ups that are characterised by a period of a constant and almost daily struggle for survival. These businesses start small and develop slowly. Due to a lack of resources and a lack of time, the entrepreneur is continually problem solving and "fire-fighting". To cope with this situation, the entrepreneur tries to leverage the scarce resources available. The decision of Anita Roddick to refill customers' bottles because she could not afford to purchase enough bottles is an example of an entrepreneur bootstrapping by turning a disadvantage into an advantage. Often entrepreneurs will rent premises and plant rather than purchase them. Staff will be hired on a part-time basis until the business can afford full-time staff. The entrepreneur may seek help from family and friends.

"Boom or Bust"

"Boom or Bust" businesses require a large up-front commitment of resources and often expenditure on specialised assets. It is not possible for the entrepreneur to start small and gradually develop the business. These businesses must develop enough sales to fund the large capital investments made at start-up. If targeted sales are not achieved, the business fails; however, if the business is successful, it will normally be quite large and profitable. An example of this type of business would be building a whiskey distillery or the development of a large-scale tourist attraction. These projects require large capital investments and therefore must achieve large sales to cover the investment.

Managing a Start-up
The overall objective of the entrepreneur at start-up is to establish the business in the market. The entrepreneur will spend all of the start-up period managing and solving short-term problems. A well-prepared business plan can be an essential guide to the entrepreneur during this period. The business plan provides the entrepreneur with a set of objectives and actions. Additionally, it provides a mechanism for comparing actual performance with expected performance. The main areas of activity that the entrepreneur needs to pay particular attention to during the launch period are:

- Resource acquisition
- Getting ready for business
- Producing the product/service

- Getting customers and establishing a market presence
- Managing finance and monitoring performance

Resource Acquisition

The entrepreneur will spend most of the time prior to start-up acquiring the resources that are needed. In some businesses, these must all be in place prior to start-up — for example a restaurant must be fully fitted and staff must be hired and trained prior to opening. Entrepreneurs may rent or borrow equipment rather than purchase it.

Getting Ready for Business

The day-to-day problems associated with getting ready to do business will take most of the entrepreneur's time. The entrepreneur will have to deal with issues such as getting the telephone connected, buying stock and supplies, and equipping the premises. Many problems will be encountered and often the entrepreneur will fall behind schedule. This can be very costly, as the business will be incurring costs without producing any revenues.

Producing the Product / Service

The entrepreneur must begin production of the product/service. During the first few months of business, it is essential that the entrepreneur manages both the cost of producing the product/ service and the quality of the product/service. As the business expands and sales increase, the attention that each individual order receives may decrease and quality may slip.

Getting Customers and Establishing a Market Presence

The objective of the launch period is to get the business established. The most essential element of this is to inform potential customers of the business and to get them to try the product or service. Where possible, the entrepreneur should make use of free publicity associated with the launch of the business. The entrepreneur faces a number of challenges in trying to build up a customer base. The entrepreneur has to persuade potential customers to try the product. During the initial few months of a new business sales may be satisfactory due to friends and business contacts supporting the start-up. These initial customers are referred to as "soft" customers. These initial orders will have to be developed into repeat orders. In most businesses, it is repeat orders and purchases that keep the business alive. Having got the customer to buy the product/service, the entrepreneur must ensure that payment is received. Additionally, the entrepreneur should monitor the price of the product/service and how competitors have reacted. Competitors may react by putting pressure on suppliers, distributors and buyers not to deal with the new business.

 Managing Finance and Monitoring Performance

Cash management is the most important issue during start-up. Cash is the lifeblood of a new business. Most businesses fail due to poor financial management. Many good ideas that have been proven in the market place have failed due to poor cash management. Monitoring performance during start-up is critical. Most entrepreneurs are weak in this area and get so caught up in the day-to-day running of the business that they lose sight of the overall direction and performance of the business. In an effort to get sales, many entrepreneurs ignore the necessity of managing the credit process. The entrepreneur must pay close attention to the management of cash and, in particular, the generation of cash. The performance of the business should be compared to the budgets in the business plan. Accounting packages that operate on a PC can help the entrepreneur control the performance of the new business.

Barriers to a Successful Launch

Despite all the planning done prior to start-up, many things will go wrong. The problems that the start-up is likely to experience include:

- **Lack of Resources**: The new business will only survive if it acquires the financial, human and physical resources it needs. Failure to secure all the funding needed may create cash flow problems for the business. Some businesses find it difficult to acquire the premises and equipment they need.

- **Overcoming Customer Inertia**: Customers will usually have an existing supplier. Changing supplier and/or trying a new product/service involve a risk. The power of existing brands and brand image can make it difficult for entrepreneurs to persuade customers that the new product/service is better. Satisfied customers may not be interested in investing time to consider a new product/service. Even if customers can be persuaded to try the product, the entrepreneur may have to change a buying pattern and habit.

- **Overcoming Competitors**: Most markets are supplied by a number of competitors. Competitors may react to a new entrant by reducing prices or increasing expenditure on sales and promotion. Alternatively, existing competitors may try to restrict access to distribution channels or access to suppliers.

- **Achieving Satisfactory Margins**: Inevitably during start-up, costs overrun budgets. There are many costs that the entrepreneur did not anticipate. A combination of higher costs and lower sales prices due to the reaction of competitors may result in lower margins.

- **Getting Paid**: Sales will be slow to develop and converting credit sales into cash may be a very slow and difficult process. The entrepreneur may be slow to put pressure on customers for payment because of a fear that subsequent business may be lost. Also the entrepreneur may not have a credit control process or payment collection procedure in the company. The lack of these systems may slow down the flow of cash into the business.

- **Time**: The entrepreneur will find that there is not enough time to get everything done and that things take longer than planned. Delays can be costly for a new business. Delays may be the result of poor and unrealistic expectations about the business. The preparation of a business plan should help the entrepreneur overcome these problems. Inevitably, there will be some time delays that the entrepreneur cannot anticipate or control.

O'Farrell (1986) identified the main problems that Irish manufacturing businesses experience at start-up.

- **Obtaining Working Capital**: Working capital problems arise due to bad debts, slowness of payments, high interest rates.

- **Obtaining Medium- and Long-term Finance**: Difficulty in getting access to finance at a reasonable interest rate. Most entrepreneurs are resistant to the idea of selling equity to raise finance for the business.

- **Obtaining Suitable Premises**: Difficulty in getting suitable premises at an acceptable price.

- **Obtaining Payment**: Entrepreneurs find it difficult to get payment from customers.

- **Getting Credit from Suppliers**: Suppliers may be slow to extend credit facilities to a new company. Cash on delivery requirements put added strain on the cash flow of a business.

- **Lack of Demand**: Interestingly, this was not high on the list of problems.

CHOOSING A STRATEGY

A new business should have both a competitive strategy and a mar-ket-entry strategy. These decisions should be based on an under-standing and an analysis of customers and competitors. The strategy of the business should be explained and justified in the business plan.

Market-entry Strategy

The market share and market coverage of a company such as O2 (previously Esat Digifone) is very different from that of a new local video store. Market-entry strategy refers to how the new business will enter the market. A new business may choose to enter only one market segment or one geographic market, or alternatively it may choose to enter the whole market. The decision on which market-entry strategy to use is determined by a number of factors:

- **Resources**. New businesses with limited resources will usually choose to concentrate these resources in a limited number of market or geographic segments. They will enter one market segment and, over time, develop into other segments of the market.

- **Capital Investment and Scale Requirements**. Industries that have large economies of scale favour larger businesses. A new entrant must attempt to get sufficient volume quickly. Often this volume will only be achievable if the whole market is entered.

- **Product Life Cycle**. If the product/service has a short life cycle, the entrepreneur will need to grow the business quickly and may be more likely to enter with a broad market-entry strategy. The software industry is an example of a sector where the entrepreneur will probably have to maximise sales of the product quickly.

- **Proprietary Protection**. If the product/service lacks any proprietary protection such as patents or trade secrets, the entrepreneur will seek to get maximum sales before competitors imitate the product/service.

- **Market Structure and Competition**. The more competitive and saturated a market, the more difficult it is for a new entrant to achieve sales.

Figure *2.8: Cooley Distillery: Entering the World Whiskey Industry*

Cooley Distillery was set-up by two Irish entrepreneurs in September 1987 to produce and sell an independent Irish whiskey. Prior to this, the production and sale of Irish whiskey had been monopolised by Irish Distillers Group, owned by the international drinks company, Pernod-Ricard. Despite a long tradition as a whiskey-producing country, Irish whiskey has only a 1% share of the world whiskey market. Under Irish law whiskey must be matured for at least three years before it can be called "Irish whiskey".

In 1991, John Teeling, one of the founders, began to seek an outside partner, to provide both additional capital and access to distribution channels. He encountered difficulties in attracting a partner and, due to the lack of financial resources, Cooley Distillery ceased production of its whiskey in February 1993. Cooley's worsening financial situation persuaded the original investors and management to abandon their dream of creating an independent Irish whiskey brand. Teeling began negotiations to sell out to Irish Distillers Group. IDG launched a €27.93 million bid for Cooley and publicly announced its intention to close down the company. IDG justified the proposed closure on the grounds that the Cooley Distillery might "damage the reputation of Irish whiskey" in overseas markets. In March 1994, the Irish Competition Authority blocked the bid on the grounds it was anti-competitive.

Teeling put together a €2.41 million rescue package. The Cooley project was now "two years late, has higher whiskey costs, and is left carrying over €1.27 million in losses" (Cooley Annual Report, 1994). During the negotiations with IDG, all distribution deals, marketing plans and the production of whiskey had been put on hold. Cooley made the decision to "to go on our own" and now faces the difficult challenge of breaking into the world whiskey market. The options identified include supplying quality whiskey products to:

- *New whiskey markets in South America, Asia and Eastern Europe*
- *Multiples in traditional whiskey markets interested in "own label" products*
- *Existing whiskey drinkers in mature whiskey markets who are seeking new taste sensations in Irish whiskey.*

"Niche" Market-entry Strategy

A niche market-entry strategy involves the entrepreneur targeting the product/service at specific market segments. The advantages of such a strategy are that the entrepreneur can conserve limited resources and ensure that all attention is given to the chosen market segment. The dangers of a niche strategy are that the entrepreneur may not achieve sufficient sales to support the business, that is the chosen market niche may be too small for the business to survive. The choice of a niche strategy may be a factor that limits the growth of a business in a small domestic market like Ireland. Small Irish businesses may have to become involved in risky and expensive export markets at an early stage.

The entrepreneur should pursue a niche strategy only if it confers a competitive advantage on the business. Otherwise, a more broadly-based strategy is preferable. For example, the market for carbonated orange drinks is unlikely to be a niche market. Customers do not identify this product as any different from other soft drinks. Competitors supplying a wider range of products, for example, lemon drinks, cola drinks, apple drinks, will have an advantage due to lower overall production, distribution and promotion costs.

"Broad" Market-entry Strategy

The entrepreneur might try to gain a large share of the market from start-up. New businesses such as Esat Digifone or Disneyland-Paris entered the market with very high market share objectives. The advantage of a broad market-entry strategy is that, if the business is successful, it will be large from the beginning. A broad market-entry strategy is often more attractive to distributors, retailers and consumers as it suggests that there will be continuity in the business. Most new businesses do not have the resources to pursue such a strategy and therefore start on a small scale. Some new businesses must pursue a broad entry strategy because of the large capital investment required at start-up. A business may pursue a broad market-entry strategy by licensing or franchising the business. Some businesses will out-source manufacturing so that resources can be concentrated on marketing and sales.

Competitive Strategy

Competitive strategy refers to how the new business will compete with existing suppliers of the product/service. A new business must either provide a better service than competitors or must provide the same service at a lower cost. There are numerous ways in which a business can deliver a better service. Many entrepreneurs fail to understand their market and customers and as a consequence don't develop a strong competitive advantage. They adopt a "me-too" strategy. This means that they replicate what has been done before without improving it.

"Lower Cost" Strategy

A "lower cost" strategy involves offering a product/service to consumers at a price less than competitors. Most entrepreneurs believe that this strategy will be successful. Their logic is that customers should be willing to pay less for the same product/service. The advantage of this strategy is that the new business should be able to attract customers. The lower price should encourage customers to try the product/service and may encourage new customers into the market. To pursue this strategy profitably, the new business must have a lower cost base than competitors. However, this strategy is not that easy to pursue and many entrepreneurs fail to pursue it successfully with the result that the business achieves low profits. There are a number of reasons why this strategy may not work for the small business:

- **Miscalculating Costs and Overheads**. The entrepreneur may not have identified all of the overheads that the business will incur. Many small businesses achieve lower overheads by operating outside the tax system or by not costing their own time at the market rate. As the business grows, overheads will increase and prices may have to be increased.

- **Customer Perceptions**. For many products, the price charged is assumed by customers to be a reflection of the quality of the product. Low prices may be interpreted by customers as a lower quality service rather than as a more efficient supplier. To overcome this problem, it might be necessary for the entrepreneur to inform customers why they are cheaper, for example, "cheaper because we buy direct from the factory". Power City, the electrical retailer, successfully pursues a low cost strategy by maximising their volumes and passing on the benefits of bulk purchases to customers.

- **Customer Requirements**. For many products, customers are more interested in better quality and better service. Increasingly, consumers are prepared to pay premium prices to businesses that will deliver a high quality product/service.

- **Failure to Advertise**. The entrepreneur may incorrectly assume that a low cost strategy means not investing in marketing and selling costs. The net effect of this is that the customer is unaware of the lower cost alternative and the new business remains small. Many small businesses fail to generate revenues to invest in advertising and promotion because of their low prices and low turnover. Ryanair successfully pursues a low cost strategy by ensuring that the cost of providing their service is minimised yet they spend heavily on advertising and promotion.

- **Competitor Response**. New competitors with lower costs may enter the market. Often these are overseas competitors that operate in low wage countries or new businesses that do not understand the full cost of operating in this business.

"Better Service" Strategy

A "better service" strategy involves offering a better product or service to consumers at an acceptable price. There are many ways in which a business may have a better product/service. These include superior product/service performance, faster delivery service, better location, wider product range, personal advice and after-sales service, longer credit terms, more flexible service, personalised attention. It is important that the entrepreneur tries to maximise the number and the extent of these advantages. This strategy is often not successful for several reasons:

- **Customer Requirements**. Often the "better" service/product that the new business is offering is not of value to customers.

- **Poor Pricing**. To get the benefits of a better product/service, the new business should be able to charge a similar or higher price. Most new businesses claim that they offer a superior product/service than their competitors. However, despite this better product/service, these businesses will claim that they are also more price-competitive.

- **Poor Promotion**. Often new businesses fail to communicate their better product/service to their customers. This may be because promotion, advertising and sales support expenditures are often wrongly considered by the entrepreneur to be a luxury.

STRATEGIES FOR SUCCESS IN SMALL AND MEDIUM-SIZED IRISH COMPANIES[6]

A survey of successful Irish companies revealed that there are common strategies pursued by successful companies. The study analysed 131 small and medium-sized manufacturing and services businesses. Success was defined as the ability of the company to grow consistently over a five-year period. The study suggests that those small companies that wish to be successful must pay special attention to the decisions they make with regard to market choice (industry, sector, segment) and competitive strategy. The results of this research suggest that the first key managerial choice is "where to compete" but that this is followed by a second key choice, which is about "how to compete". It is the combination of these that results in success. Some important implications flow from this:

- Market choice is a critical managerial decision. It is not, however, a choice that is, or can be, subject to frequent change. Market selection will always be constrained by the entrepreneur's experiences.

- The choice of market determines the likelihood of success and growth. If the "wrong" market is chosen, then success will be limited or unachievable.

- Choosing a growing market is not a sufficient condition for successful growth. Other decisions will influence whether a business achieves success in its market.

Specifically, the study identified a number of competitive and growth strategies. These were that successful companies:

- **Compete in High Growth Markets**. Successful companies compete in markets with higher growth rates. The mean growth rate of the successful companies' markets was approximately three times that for low growth companies (Figure 2.9).

- **Focus on Market Niches**. The average size of the market that the successful companies competed in was about half the size of the market that the less successful companies competed in. The smaller size of the market competed in is interpreted as an indication of a market niche strategy. However, within these niche markets, the successful companies were more likely to have a

---

[6] See Murray, J. & C. O'Gorman (1994): "Growth strategies for the smaller business", *Journal of Strategic Change*, Vol. 3, 127, 1–9.

wider product range. This was unexpected because it was thought that, as part of their focus strategy, high-growth companies would be characterised by a narrow product range. A possible explanation for this is that the small size of the Irish market requires Irish companies to cover all product options in their niche.

- **Compete on the Uniqueness of their Product**. Successful companies were more likely to have products that were differentiated from their competitors'.

- **Provide Superior Product Quality and Superior Customer Service**. Relative to competitors, successful companies were more likely to sell higher quality products and to have a higher customer service reputation.

- **Are Innovative**. Innovation was measured by the percentage of a company's sales that came from new products. Relative to their competitors, successful companies had a higher percentage of new products.

- **Build on their Strengths**. Successful companies grew by emphasising their existing strengths and by developing into related markets.

Figure 2.9: Mean Percentage Served Market Growth Rate

Year	Successful Companies	All Companies
1987–88	9.8	5.1
1988–89	11.5	6.8
1989–90	11.5	8.1

CONCLUSION

This chapter has highlighted that there are many different ways to become an entrepreneur. However the problems experienced by many entrepreneurs during the launch of a new business are quite similar. The success of a new business is dependent on identifying a competitive strategy and a market-entry strategy. Many new businesses fail to explicitly develop these strategies and suffer, as a consequence, from low profitability.

QUESTIONS

1. Describe the different ways of becoming an entrepreneur. Illustrate your answer with examples.
2. What problems will a business experience during the launch period? How might an entrepreneur cope with these problems?
3. What market-entry strategies are available to a small business?
4. Why do many small businesses fail to implement their competitive strategy effectively?
5. Identify the reasons for the success of a small business in your locality.
6. In a group, identify the competitive strategies and the competitive advantage of five businesses.

REFERENCES

O'Farrell, P. (1986): *Entrepreneurs and Industrial Change*, Dublin: IMI.

Kuratko, D. and Welsch, P., (2001): *Strategic Entrepreneurial Growth*, Orlando, FL: Harcourt Publishers.

3

THE BUSINESS PLAN

INTRODUCTION

Why should an entrepreneur go to the trouble of writing a business plan? The simple answer is that starting a business is difficult and the entrepreneur must manage a wide range of different activities. The process of preparing a plan forces the entrepreneur to think through the different aspects of the new venture. Having completed the business plan, the entrepreneur should have identified the market opportunity and how it is to be exploited. Specifically, the entrepreneur must develop an entry strategy and a competitive strategy.

The first part of this chapter discusses why the entrepreneur should write a business plan and details where the entrepreneur should get the required information. This is followed by an outline of the format of a business plan. Each section of the business plan is discussed in detail. Chapter 4 contains an example of a business plan for a restaurant.

MUST THE ENTREPRENEUR WRITE THE PLAN?

The entrepreneur is the person best placed to produce a meaningful plan. By preparing a business plan, the entrepreneur ensures that there is a viable business opportunity. The business plan can reduce the financial and personal risk involved in starting a new business. The entrepreneur is taking the risk and therefore should be involved in the preparation of the business plan. The disadvantage of outsourcing the preparation of the business plan is that the entrepreneur loses out on some of the benefits of engaging in the planning process.

However, entrepreneurs do not always prepare their own business plan. The preparation of a business plan is a difficult and time-consuming process and many entrepreneurs seek external assistance when preparing one. The entrepreneur may get an outsider to write the complete plan, to prepare the financial information or simply to help gather market information. Where the entrepreneur sees the plan essentially as a document for raising finance or an unnecessary burden imposed by an external financing agency, it is more likely that an outsider will be used. Some entrepreneurs will pay an outsider to prepare the business plan because they believe they lack the management skills to prepare the plan themselves. In a survey of entrepreneurs who prepared business plans, one entrepreneur explained that at an early stage he used external agents to do some planning for him, because he "imagined" that there was some skill involved which could only be "bought in". However, on seeing the contribution of the external advisors, the entrepreneur prepared all his own plans in future.

Figure 3.1: Dos & Don'ts in Writing a Business Plan

- Keep the plan short, simple and concise.
- Keep your plan focused. Don't be over ambitious at the start.
- Forecast sales based on market information.
- Justify your claims and avoid unsubstantiated statements, for example, "there are no competitors", "this is a huge market", etc.
- Use simple language as readers of the business plan may not understand technical jargon. They may question your ability to sell the product if you can't communicate to them.
- Don't have surprises. Identify potential problems and name all investors.

Who Will Read the Business Plan?
The plan will be read by a variety of people, each of whom may be interested in different aspects of the document. The entrepreneur may use the business plan to raise capital from private investors, financial institutions, and state agencies. The plan may be used to attract a potential partner into the business and to gain creditability with potential customers and suppliers. Therefore, the plan needs to be comprehensive enough to address each of their particular concerns. Some entrepreneurs prepare separate plans for themselves and for external readers of the plan. The "internal" document might address issues that the entrepreneur believes are best kept secret from potential investors and lenders. A list of people who are likely to read the plan is outlined in Figure 3.2.

Figure 3.2: Readers and their Interest in the Business Plan

Lending Institutions, State Agencies and Venture Capitalists
Funding Requirement; Cash Flow Projections; Proposed Market; Level of Risk Involved; Costings and Pricing; Financial Viability; Industry Structure and Competition; Entrepreneurs' Experience.

Customers
Quality Issues; Product Functionality; After Sales Service; Warranties; Product Range.

Suppliers
Order Quantity; Frequency of Orders; Payment Terms; Product Design; Financial Strength.

Senior Managers/Partners
Required Equity Investment; Pay Structure; Levels of Responsibilities; Promotion.

Where to Get the Information?

When preparing a business plan, the entrepreneur must identify the critical pieces of information required to evaluate the market and plan the business. The entrepreneur should identify what information will be needed, where this information can be sourced, and how this information is to be analysed and presented in the business plan. The most difficult information to identify is the size of the potential market and the position of competitors in the market. Figure 3.3 lists the principal information that the entrepreneur will have to collect.

The most important source of information for many entrepreneurs is their personal experience of working in the sector. Information is central to making a decision on whether there is a viable business opportunity and how best this opportunity can be exploited. The process of gathering information and evaluating a business opportunity is often unsystematic and haphazard. Most entrepreneurs will use their contacts in business to gather specific pieces of information they may need and to get advice on their proposed business.

Figure 3.3: Principal Information Requirements

- Market size, industry sector size.
- A demographic profile of the target market/customers.
- Trends in market, technology, consumers' tastes and preferences.
- Competitor profiling: number, size, strengths and weaknesses.
- Profitability in the sector.
- Barriers to entry.
- Pricing policies, promotion and advertising practices.
- Proposed location: size, facilities, rents and activity patterns.
- Appropriate channels of distribution.

An entrepreneur may use **secondary sources of data to get back-ground information on the sector.** This is common when the entrepreneur is new to the business and when the concept is new. Secondary data can be **gathered from published reports, newspapers, specialist/trade magazine articles, and statistics that** have been compiled by other people for a variety of purposes. These sources should be used by the entrepreneur to identify past and current trends and events in the business sector. The information obtained from secondary sources is often limited due to its broad nature. Figure 3.4 lists the sources of secondary information.

Figure 3.4: Sources of Secondary Information

- Libraries: Local Authorities and University Libraries.
- Government and EU Agencies.
- Enterprise Boards and Partnership Companies.
- The Registrar of Companies.
- Central Statistics Office.
- Chambers of Commerce.
- Trade Associations and Journals.
- Websites (OECD, World Bank, *The Economist* etc).

Once the entrepreneur has built up a picture of what is happening in
the particular market, **primary sources of information** may be used.
Primary sources of information are gathered by going out to talk to
the various players in the market place, such as competitors, customers, suppliers, experts, etc. How should the entrepreneur approach
this task? The entrepreneur should speak directly with potential customers and where possible get a commitment to buy from the new
business. Commitments from customers can help the entrepreneur
persuade an investor to lend money to the new business. The entrepreneur should visit competitors and collect material about their
product/service. This may be possible by attending a trade fair and
pretending to be a potential customer. Some entrepreneurs work in
the particular industry to gain valuable experience in order to fully
understand the operations of a business, and then start-up their venture. Industry experts can offer some valuable overviews on the developments within specific sectors.

THE BUSINESS PLAN

Figure 3.5: Table of Contents of the Business Plan

---

1. Executive Summary
1.1 Principals involved in the Venture
1.2 The Product/Service
1.3 Target Market
1.4 Level of Profitability
1.5 Funding Requirement and Return on Investment

2. Description of the Product/Service

3. Industry and Competitor Analysis
3.1 Political, Economic, Social and Technological Trends
3.2 Market Opportunities and Threats
3.3 Industry Structure
3.4 Competitor Profiles

4. Marketing Plan
4.1 Market Size and Market Segments
4.2 Customer Profile and Behaviour
4.3 Market Research
4.4 Marketing Strategy
4.4.1 Positioning Strategy
4.4.2 Pricing Strategy
4.4.3 Distribution Strategy

Executive Summary

This is the first section of the business plan and it should be short and concise. The executive summary outlines the opportunity for the venture, why the opportunity exists and how the entrepreneurial team intends to exploit this opportunity. It should describe the proposed business and justify how the business will achieve its sales targets. The executive summary should outline the funding requirements and the expected return on the required investment. This is crucially important, as it is the first part that a banker or investor will read. Prospective investors will read the summary quickly to determine whether the venture is of interest and may decide to read no further. Consequently, the layout, format and presentation of the executive summary are crucial. The summary is usually the last section of the business plan to be written.

Description of Business

This section of the business plan should outline in detail the business that the entrepreneur proposes to start. This is important because outsiders may not have the background knowledge or be as familiar with the concept as the entrepreneur. Often entrepreneurs fail to explain their ideas in a comprehensive manner because they wrongly assume that others will quickly grasp the business idea. This description should enable the reader of the plan to ascertain the size and scope of the venture, the proposed product/service that will be offered, where the business will be located, who will purchase the product and why they choose this service in preference to alternatives. If appropriate, the entrepreneur should include a sample of the product, for example a copy of the menu for a restaurant business.

Industry and Competitor Analysis

In this section, the entrepreneur analyses the factors impacting on the growth and development of the target market and the competitors currently operating in the market. The purpose of this analysis is to assess the attractiveness of the target market and to identify any constraints or pressures that may exist. The entrepreneur should understand the factors that are driving the growth and development of the market. The analysis of competitors should identify their current market position and their competitive strengths.

Having completed an industry and competitor analysis, the entrepreneur should be able to answer the following questions:

- Why does this opportunity exist?
- What threats does the new business face?
- What determines the level of profitability in the industry?
- Who are the competitors and what position have they adopted?
- The size of the market and the potential sales of the new business.

There are a number of models the entrepreneur might use to structure this analysis. These techniques include STEP analysis, SWOT analysis, Porter's Five Forces model and Competitor Profiling. In using these models, the entrepreneur must be pragmatic. The models are tools to assist the entrepreneur in answering questions about the business opportunity and the strategy the new business should pursue. The entrepreneur must not become over-involved in analysis as this may delay the making of decisions. Undertaking an industry and competitor analysis can be a time-consuming process. The difficulties that an entrepreneur may face in undertaking such an analysis are outlined in Figure 3.6.

Figure 3.6: Problems in Undertaking an Industry Analysis

- **Defining Industry Boundaries Incorrectly**: An entrepreneur might fail to define the firm's industry and its boundaries properly.
- **Poor Identification of Competitors**: The venture might concentrate on local competition and ignore national or international competitors.
- **Poor Definition of Invisible Capabilities**: This is where the firm fails to focus on competitors' intangible resources. Some of these invisible factors may account for competitors' success in a given market.
- **Paralysis by Analysis**: This is where a venture carries out thorough analysis, but this thoroughness and striving to gain more information to reduce the uncertainty may mean the venture does not make any decisions in relation to its own operations.
- **Inaccurate Assumption about Competition:** The venture makes certain assumptions about competitors' operations. These assumptions may not be substantiated and may be inaccurate.
- **Getting Information**: The entrepreneur may not have the time or resources to gather the information required to start-up the venture.

STEP Analysis

The STEP (Social, Technical, Economic, Political) model assists the entrepreneur in thinking about the broader issues that have created the new business opportunity. The output of a STEP analysis should be the key factors that have created the market opportunity and a listing of the key external factors that will impact on new business.

- **Social factors**: The business plan should highlight the social factors that have created this opportunity and which explain the nature of demand in the market place. Factors such as population size, demographic structures, type of lifestyles, the culture and values of the population and the degree of segmentation in the market are of particular importance. The changing demographic profile of the Irish population is creating a number of opportunities, for example, private third level colleges, health services for the elderly.

- **Technological factors**: The entrepreneur should assess how technological developments will impact of the development of this market. These developments may create an opportunity for the entrepreneur. Additionally, the entrepreneur must identify what are the minimal technological requirements of the venture. Technological developments have created opportunities for new businesses, such as Irish businesses selling shamrocks, holidays, and electrical goods over the Internet.

- **Economic factors**: Economic factors may limit the potential of the proposed venture. Issues such as inflation rates, spending patterns, consumer confidence, strength of national currency, interest rates, sustainability of current economic activity, must be examined. Ultimately, these factors will affect how much capital the business can afford to borrow. In times of growing economic prosperity and higher incomes, there are opportunities for new luxury and high quality products.

- **Political factors**: Political and legal factors may create opportunities or difficulties for the proposed business. For example, the decision by the European Union to deregulate the airline industry created the opportunity conditions that lead to the establishment of Ryanair.

SWOT Analysis

SWOT is an acronym for Strengths, Weaknesses, Opportunities and Threats. Opportunities are the factors in the external environment that the new business will act on. The opportunities might be changes in consumer tastes and preferences that mean that consumers are demanding a new product. Threats are the external factors that may impact negatively on the new business. Threats could be the level of competition or changes in technology. The strengths and weaknesses refer to the new business itself. Strengths and weaknesses are internally-focused, whereas opportunities and threats are externally-focused. Strengths are things that the new venture will do well – for example, the experience of the entrepreneur, access to a prime retail location, access to an overseas supplier, etc. Weaknesses are areas in which the new venture will be at a competitive disadvantage.

Porter's Five Forces

Porter's (1985) Five Forces Model identifies the competitive nature of the industry. The factors in this model explain the level of profitability in the industry and who has the competitive strength. There are five key areas to consider when undertaking an industry analysis:

- **Competition**: This is at the heart of the model and is concerned with the nature and the level of rivalry among existing competitors, the number of competitors and the level of differentiation in the industry.

- **Suppliers**: What is the power of suppliers to the industry? Usually if there is a smaller number of suppliers or if they have some scarce resource, they will be in a more powerful position and will be able to charge higher prices.

- **Buyers**: What is the power of buyers in the industry? Buyer power increases as they learn more about a product. An example of this is that PCs have become commodity-type purchases as people become more knowledgeable about them. When buyers are concentrated relative to suppliers, for example, supermarkets relative to many small companies, they tend to be more powerful.

- **Potential Entrants**: The ease of entry into a market affects overall profitability levels in an industry. Industries that have high barriers to entry tend to be more profitable. Barriers to entry include the need for large scale (in cement manufacturing), the need to invest in building a brand image (in the drinks industry), and access to distribution (in the motor fuels industry).

- **Substitutes**: Are there substitute products for the current product or service? Substitute products are not competitive products but products that could potentially compete if prices fell or if performance increased. For example, plasma televisions are currently about five to 10 times more expensive than existing televisions. As the technology develops and costs reduce, these televisions will compete directly with existing products.

As an example of Porter's model, consider the soft drinks industry. The soft drinks industry is very profitable. Strong brands place the soft drinks manufacturers in a strong position relative to retailers as the retailer must stock a brand such as Coca-Cola. Suppliers to the soft drinks are not important as the raw materials of water, sugar and flavouring are readily available. The large investment necessary to build up a brand image and to get access to distribution channels reduces the threat of new entrants and reduces overall competition. There are no obvious substitute products. Competition is predominately based on marketing; Pepsi and Coke avoid price competition where possible. All of these factors help to maintain profitability for producers of branded soft drinks. However this is a dynamic situation and the introduction of Virgin Cola and "quality" own label soft drinks by retailers such as Sainsburys in the UK, Dunnes Stores in Ireland and other leading retailers has changed the nature of competition and the attractiveness of the business.

Competitor Profiling

This involves assessing the other competitors in the target market. The entrepreneur should profile each competitor on the following:

- Size and market share position
- Competitive strategy
- Strengths and weaknesses
- Image and reputation
- Assumptions regarding how the industry operates
- Financial position.

An important aspect of industry and competitor analysis is an analysis of competitors' intangible resources. These resources may be essential to competitive success. Examples of intangible resources are:

- Trade marks
- Patents
- Copyright
- Registered designs
- Contracts
- Trade secrets
- Reputation
- Networks.

Marketing Plan

Having analysed the industry and competitors, the entrepreneur must estimate the size of the market and the level of sales that the new business can expect to achieve in the first three years of business. This is the most difficult part of a business plan. The level of sales that the business achieves will determine the overall viability of the venture. The sales forecasts for the new business should be based on the understanding of the factors determining demand and the competitors in the industry. For some business opportunities, there are no existing competitors or sales. This makes the task of estimating demand even more difficult. One solution is to identify a broadly similar business and estimate their sales. The remaining sections of the business plan and the financing of the business are based on these estimated sales. Estimates of market size and potential sales should be checked by talking to potential customers.

The marketing plan should outline the overall marketing strategy of the new business. The plan should answer the following questions:

- Who will buy the product/service?
- What do they want?
- How do they decide?
- Where do they buy?
- When do they buy?
- Why do they buy?

To answer these questions, the entrepreneur will need to decide who the target market is, what benefits the product/service offers, the price of the product/service, how it will be advertised, and how the product will be distributed.

The marketing plan is regarded as a critical element to the success of the new venture. Therefore the entrepreneur has to ensure that the overall marketing strategy can be effectively implemented.

Price

The entrepreneur has to decide what price should be charged for the product/service. A number of factors should be considered when determining the price of the product:

- The price of competing products
- The cost of producing the product/service
- The level of profitability needed to repay investors and to reward the entrepreneur
- The expectations of consumers
- The image of the product
- The mark-up that wholesalers, distributors and retailers will take.

Product pricing is a difficult process and, in many small businesses, the entrepreneur will not know the actual costs associated with the manufacture of products. The number of units produced will determine the cost per unit and the entrepreneur will not know what level of sales will be achieved. In order to introduce the product onto the market, the entrepreneur may have to use discounts to encourage consumers to try the product or retailers to stock the product. Many entrepreneurs undercharge for their products, assuming that price is the most important purchasing criteria and the only source of competitive advantage. Some small businesses have increased profitability by increasing prices. This may result in lower sales but satisfied customers may continue to support the business.

Sales Methods

The entrepreneur has to decide what sales tactics will be used. Some of the options include:

- Direct selling by the entrepreneur
- Employing a sales team
- Using telephone or direct mailing
- Using an agent.

The sales method chosen will have a direct impact on the cost base of the firm, the level of service and quality delivered to customers and the degree of market penetration that will be achieved.

Promotion

How will the venture try to gain the attention of prospective purchasers? This element of the plan should outline which advertising media the entrepreneur intends to use. The options include local/national radio, newspapers, TV, Internet, direct mail shots, trade shows, advertisements in trade/industry magazines and sponsorship. The choice of media will depend on the customers being targeted. The plan should outline the entrepreneur's plans to develop promotional materials. This element of the marketing plan should outline the media to be used, the costs of this promotion and a schedule for the promotion and advertising campaign.

Distribution Channels

This section of the plan outlines where the product will be sold and the number of companies or individuals who are to be used to distrib-

ute it. The entrepreneur will have to decide **whether the product** will
be sold directly to the customer or through a channel. An important
consideration is the **image of the product/service.** The two over-riding
considerations for the entrepreneur are the level of customer convenience and the efficiency of the distribution channel.

Customer Care

The venture has to establish a procedure for generating and dealing
with customer enquiries. The entrepreneur **should have some system**
for ensuring customers are satisfied with their purchases. Often this
can be done informally by talking to customers.

In addition, **the venture may provide an after-sales service to customers such as a warranty or guarantee.** The entrepreneur has to
consider what competitors offer in terms of **warranties and after sales**
service and to decide if they are going to offer the same or additional
warranties. The entrepreneur should also consider if the company
will charge customers a call out fee for this service or whether the
cost of the service should be included in the price of the product.

Production Plan

If the proposed business is going to manufacture a product, a production plan is necessary.

For service businesses, the entrepreneur should prepare a plan of
how the service will be delivered to customers. For example, a service
business such as a café must make decisions about location, layout,
scheduling, etc.

The key decisions that must be made are as follows:

- **Location**: For service businesses, location is often one of the most
  important decisions. In sectors such as retailing, hotels and
  catering, the location of the business may determine its ultimate
  success. The entrepreneur is in the difficult situation that
  resources are scare and the rental and lease costs of prime
  locations may be prohibitive. However, choosing a less attractive
  location may result in less passing trade. The location of a
  manufacturing business should be decided by the geographical
  location of suppliers and customers. The plan should outline the
  size of the location and the local infrastructure facilities.

- **Production Process**: The entrepreneur should describe the
  production process and include an illustration of the production
  flow. The entrepreneur should consider whether it is essential to
  manufacture the product or could the production process be

subcontracted to another firm. In addition, the current capacity levels should be calculated.

- **Equipment Requirements**: The entrepreneur needs to identify the capital equipment required to produce the product or deliver the service. The entrepreneur might use new or second-hand equipment and may consider leasing some equipment to reduce the capital needed at start-up. The suppliers of the necessary equipment should be identified and the cost of production and installation should be calculated.

- **Sources of Raw Materials**: The quality of the goods and service bought-in by the business impacts on the quality of the finished product. Effective procurement of goods and services helps to maintain quality and to control costs. The raw materials required to produce the product/service should be identified and where possible agreements be made with suppliers. Suppliers may be slow to offer credit terms to a new business.

- **Cost of Production**: The cost of production should be calculated. These costs should be broken down into key elements such as materials, labour, and overheads. Costs should be divided into fixed costs and variable costs. Fixed costs are constant and include items such as rent and rates, heating and light, etc. Variable costs depend on the level of production and include raw materials, direct labour required to produce the product.

- **Warehousing Costs**: The entrepreneur has to consider the provisions for storage of the in-bound raw materials and the finished product and their movements. Basic warehousing breaks down into four operations: receiving the goods into the warehouse; transferring the goods from point of entry to the appropriate location in the warehouse; selecting the particular combinations of goods for customer order or raw materials for the production cycles; and preparing the goods for shipment to the customer.

- **Transport Costs**: Transport costs can be a significant expense and this can impact on the efficiency of the logistics operation, operating costs and demand for the product/service. The selection of a carrier is more than a basic procurement decision that involves evaluating the cost structures of various transportation modes. Other factors that must be considered are inventory levels due to transit times; warehouse and facility design; dependability of mode of transport; handling damage via each mode; cost of tracking shipments; and impact on facilities operating costs.

- **Quality Issues**: The entrepreneur must consider how quality is to be maintained. In some industries customers will require suppliers to have some form of quality accreditation such as ISO 9000 or the Q-Mark. The entrepreneur needs to set out the quality standards that are applicable at all stages of the manufacturing and selling process.

- **Legal Issues**: When setting up a manufacturing operation the venture is likely to have to meet many legal requirements. These include environmental approval, health permits, planning permission, etc.

Figure 3.7: Carrier and Modal Selection

The choice of transportation involves choosing a mode of transport, deciding what carrier firm to use and the modal selection:

- *Modal Choice: Carrier selection is a two-fold process. Initially, the entrepreneur selects a mode of transport given the ventures location, target market, access to the different modes. The choice of modes is rail, air, sea and road. The venture can use intermodal transport whereby it uses one or more modes to transport the product over a given route. This may mean using rail and then road or air and then using road to transport the product.*

- *Specific Carrier Selection: Once a decision has been made regarding the modal choice, then a specific carrier firm within the chosen mode or intermodal form must be selected. Can they transport the goods from the factory to the different buyers' premises? If the buyers and distribution outlets are dispersed then the entrepreneur may find it difficult to ship the products from an in-house situation.*

- *Modal Selection: This involves evaluating the rates and service levels of alternative modes and intermodal forms. Given the deregulation in the transportation environment, it is important to note that charges and service performance can vary among carriers within the same mode. Due to different market and operating conditions that different carriers face, their charges may differ. The entrepreneur should bear in mind that cost is not the most important factor in the selection of a specific carrier. The service performance of a carrier becomes a pertinent issue when determining the carrier selection.*

Human Resources and Organisational Structure

This section of the business plan should identify the management and staff requirements of the new business. It should detail who will be responsible for the different areas of activity in the business. Staff costs and remuneration levels for all employees should be calculated.

The organisational plan should contain the following information:

- **Management Personnel**: This should include CVs of the people who will hold key management positions. In addition, information regarding their duties and responsibilities, level of remuneration such as profit sharing, stock options and other bonus schemes, and employment contract periods should be included.

- **Staff Recruitment, Selection and Training**: The number of employees needed and how these will be hired. If training is necessary the entrepreneur should have a plan for this.

- **Board of Directors**: This should include information about the size and composition of the board. The advantage of a board of directors is that it provides a relatively cheap form of expert advice to the business. Also external directors might provide the business with useful contacts. The state agency, Enterprise Ireland, has recognised the advantages that outside advisors can give a business and have set up a mentor scheme for small businesses. This scheme recognises that most small and new businesses can't afford a board of directors. The Mentor Scheme gets retired senior managers to act as a "board of directors" for a small business. The mentor meets with the owner-manager about eight times a year and provides advice and a "sounding board" for ideas the entrepreneur may have.

- **Employment and Labour Legislation**: It is essential that the entrepreneur be aware of the legal rights of employees and the processes that must be followed when hiring and dismissing employees. No matter what type of business the venture operates under it will have to comply with certain health and safety regulations. Every organisation is obliged under law to produce a health and safety statement for the workplace.

- **Legal Forms of Ownership**: The entrepreneur has to decide on a legal form for the business. The entrepreneur will also have to register the name of the business with the Registry of Business Names if the entrepreneur wants to trade under a name other than their own.

Figure 3.8: Legal Forms of Business Ownership

Sole Trader

This is a where an individual trades on their own account and there is no separation between the business and the individual. The advantage of this form of ownership is that there are minimal set-up costs and legal requirements. The risks are that the owner is personally liable for all debts the business incurs.

Partnerships

A partnership is a formal relationship that exists between persons carrying on business in common with a view to a profit. Different partners usually bring various elements such as experience and finance to the business. The Partnership Agreement should deal with such matters as management of the partnership, termination of the agreement, division of profits and the level of remuneration of different partners. The advantages of setting up a partnership is that it is relatively cheap and easy to set up and there is limited level of regulation. In addition there is the advantage of a number of people sharing the risk. The disadvantage is that there is unlimited liability, which means that the partners could be liable for the debts of the business. In addition it may turn out that the partners may be incompatible. Partnerships are common among professionals such as lawyers, doctors, and accountants. They are not used in most other businesses.

Limited Liability Company

This the most common form of legal ownership of a business. Most companies are privately owned. The cost of formation can range from about €380 for an "off the shelf" company to about Euro 800 for one set up for a particular business. The other type of company is a public company. The shares of these companies can be bought and sold by the public on the Stock Exchange. Regardless of its status the limited company will have the following documents:

- **Memorandum of Association:** This outlines the type of business the company will operate.
- **Articles of Association:** This governs the internal running of the company.
- **A Minute book:** The records of the meeting of the board of directors are recorded in this.
- **A Company Seal:** This is stamped on official company documents.

> • *A Certificate of Incorporation: This is issued by the Registrar of Companies.*
>
> *The advantage of this legal form is that the owners are not liable for the debts of the business. The business is a separate legal entity. Ownership can be transferred easily and losses can be carried forward and offset against profits in prosperous years. There are many tax advantages to having a company. The downside is that there are many formalities to comply with such as filing annual returns of accounts to the Registrar of Companies.*

Financial Plan

This is probably the most critical section of the business plan. The finance section demonstrates the financial viability of the business and the level of investment required. The finance section is a financial summary of the decisions made in all the other parts of the business plan. It is important that the figures included in the finance plan are explained and that the reader understands the assumptions that the entrepreneur has made. Many entrepreneurs may find it difficult to prepare financial accounts and may employ an accountant to help them. The finance plan provides potential investors with a way of evaluating the attractiveness of the business. It also provides the entrepreneur with a set of budgets for controlling and monitoring the performance of the business during its first few years.

In writing a business plan, the entrepreneur's objective is to persuade potential investors that the business is a good investment. In raising equity finance the entrepreneur must demonstrate the ability of the business to grow so that the investor will make a capital gain. When trying to raise loan finance the entrepreneur must demonstrate the ability of the business to repay the loan. When raising finance from a bank the entrepreneur must realise that the bank will often have an "informational" advantage. The bank will often have previous experience of lending to similar ventures and will therefore be able to check to ensure that the financial projections are realistic. Also the entrepreneur should be conscious of the process that is involved in a bank considering an application for a loan. The bank will need written financial projections so that a number of individuals will be able to assess the loan proposal.

Cash management and financial control over the operations of the new business will be critical to the success of the venture. A system of control has evolved and these controls are known as financial statements. These statements are used by financiers to measure the current and future health of the business. The basic statements that the entrepreneur will use are Cash flow Forecasts, the Profit and Loss Account and the Balance Sheet. One of the objectives of these statements is demonstrate to the principals of the business how their investment capital is being utilised. In addition, the venture may have to produce audited statements that have to be filed under the Companies Act 1986.

The finance plan should include *pro forma* or forecast cash flows, profit and loss accounts and balance sheets. Additionally, it should calculate the return on investment the investor will receive and the level of sales necessary to break even. It is essential to outline what reporting procedures the venture will put in place and what actions will be undertaken if there are budget overruns. The entrepreneur must deal with the issue of taxation. The new business will have obligations to collect and pay taxes. The more important taxes a business must deal with are VAT, PAYE, PRSI, and tax on profits. There is a tendency for many start-up businesses to put taxation issues on the "long finger". It is strongly advisable that tax affairs be in order from the outset.

The Cash Flow Statement

The cash flow statement determines the demands on cash on a monthly basis and is essentially a forecast of the best estimate of all receipts and payments. This is the most important element of the finance plan. Most new businesses fail because they run out of cash. In some cases new businesses are more successful than forecast. If the business grows faster than expected it will need funds to finance stock, debtors and other items at the rate at which the business is growing. Failure to manage cash and raise additional funds may result in financial difficulties.

The statement should provide a picture of the timing and amount of cash receipts and payments. This statement is only concerned with cash flow and no allowance is made for items such as depreciation. Cash forecasting should be done monthly over a twelve-month period. Budgets should be compared to actual receipts and payments on every month. Some ventures may find large discrepancies between receipts and payments and therefore will have to prepare weekly cash flow statements. In preparing a cash flow statement there are three elements: preparing receipts, preparing payments and comparing the two forecasts to discover whether there is a surplus or a deficit during each period.

- **Cash Receipts**: The accuracy of this element of the statement will depend on the reliability of the sales forecast. It is critical that the sales forecast be accurate as it will enhance the statement. The entrepreneur must allow for credit sales.

- **Cash Payments**: This element of the statement includes all payments such as wages, light, heat, telephone, interest, taxation and loan repayments for that period, be it a month or a week.

- **Cash Surplus/Deficit**: The cash receipts minus the cash payments should reveal if the firm has a cash surplus or deficit.

The Profit and Loss Account

This is a forecast of the business's sales and expenses and the resulting profit/loss. This is usually calculated on a yearly basis but the entrepreneur should prepare quarterly profit and loss statements for the first year of the new business. The Profit and Loss Account can be divided into five broad headings:

- **Gross and Net Sales for the Period**: The differences between the two figures arise as a result of discounts, allowances and returns.

- **Cost of Goods Sold**: This figure is the cost of producing the sales. The balancing figure between net sales and cost of goods sold is the gross profit/loss for the period.

- **Selling and Distribution Expenses**: These are estimated and deducted.

- **Administration General and Interest Costs**: These are estimated and deducted.

- **Adjustment to the Final Net Profit/Loss**: Net profit/loss is gross profit/loss less expenses. This figure may need to be adjusted for tax and dividend payments.

The Balance Sheet

This is a statement of all assets and liabilities that a business has on a particular day. This is usually calculated on a yearly basis but the entrepreneur should prepare quarterly balance sheets for the first year of the new business. The balance sheet outlines the sources of funds the business will use. This statement is like a photograph as it shows the financial position of the business on a given day, and it reflects the past rather than the future. The items in the Balance Sheet will be grouped into assets, liabilities and a "financed by" section.

- **Assets:** These are the resources that the venture currently hold and can be classified into the following categories:
  - ◊ Current/Liquid Assets: These assets can be converted into cash within a twelve-month period.
  - ◊ Fixed Assets: These are usually the permanent facilities of the business that are used to produce the product/service. There is a further classification into tangible fixed assets, which include land, equipment, vehicles and buildings, and intangible fixed assets, which include goodwill, patents, trademarks and copyrights.

  Due to the fact that the assets are being used over the period, part of the income is set aside in the accounts — this is known as depreciation. The objective of depreciation is to spread the cost of the asset over its useful life.

- **Liabilities:** These are sums of money that the venture owes to others and they are grouped into the following categories:
  - ◊ Current Liabilities: Creditors, short-term loans and bank overdrafts.
  - ◊ Long-term Liabilities: This covers all the liabilities payable in more than twelve months.
  - ◊ Contingent Liabilities: These only appear in accounts in exceptional cases, for example if the venture is involved in legal proceeds and gives some form of guarantee.

- **"Financed By":** The principals' interest in the firm can be calculated by its Net Worth, that is, all assets minus all liabilities. This is usually presented in a "Financed By" or a "Net Worth" section of the Balance Sheet. It can appear as follows:
  - ◊ Issued Share Capital: This is capital/funds that has been raised from the principals of the venture.
  - ◊ Reserves: This covers the profits that have not been paid out in dividends to investors or any surpluses that have accumulated as a result of the re-valuing of assets.
  - ◊ Share Premium Account: This shows the premium, if any, that has been paid by investors to purchase further equity holding in the venture in the form of shares.

Profitability and Break-Even Analysis

Another element of the financial plan should be information on the returns that have, or that will be, achieved by the business. Profitability can be calculated in a number of ways such as return on sales and return on investment (Figure 3.10). The figures used to calculate the various profitability figures come from the Balance Sheet and the Profit and Loss Statements.

The entrepreneur should calculate the level of sales necessary to achieve break-even and the number of months that it will take before break-even is achieved (Figure 3.9). The entrepreneur should do a sensitivity analysis on all figures.

Figure 3.9: Break-even Analysis

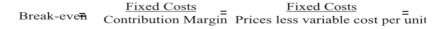

$$\text{Break-even} \quad \frac{\text{Fixed Costs}}{\text{Contribution Margin}} = \frac{\text{Fixed Costs}}{\text{Prices less variable cost per unit}} =$$

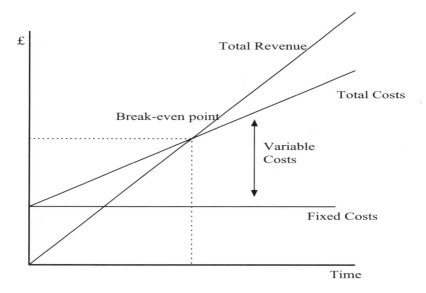

Interpretation of Financial Accounts

Ratio analysis involves comparing one figure against another to calculate a ratio. This calculation of a ratio is then used to assess the venture's current financial strengths and weaknesses. Venture capitalists, potential investors and other stakeholders use financial ratios to assess how the business is performing. These ratios may be used to compare it over time or to other businesses in the same sector.

The broad categories of ratios are profitability, short- and long-term liquidity, gearing and investment ratios (Figure 3.11). Under each category there are a number of ratios that can be calculated.

Figure 3.10: Profitability and Investment Ratios

- **Rate of Return of Capital Employed**: This ultimately indicates the success or failure of the business:

$$\frac{\text{Net profit before interest and tax}}{\text{Capital employed}}$$

- **Return on Shareholders' Investment**: This is another measure of the return on shareholders investment:

$$\frac{\text{Net profit before tax}}{\text{Share capital and reserves}}$$

- **Gross Profit as a Percentage of Sales**: This indicates the percentage of sales remaining after paying for the cost of goods sold. Obviously the higher the percentage/margin the better:

$$\frac{\text{Gross Profit}}{\text{Sales}} \quad X \quad 100$$

- **Net Profit as a Percentage of Sales**: This indicates the percentage margin of profit left after all the costs have been deducted from net sales:

$$\frac{\text{Net Profit}}{\text{Sales}} \quad X \quad 100$$

Critical Risks

In this section, the entrepreneur should identify and outline the key risks associated with the new business. These may be external events that the business has no control over. The entrepreneur should outline how the business might cope with these external shocks. Not to include these problems in the business plan runs the risk of losing credibility with potential investors. An investor who is aware of a potential problem or risk and finds no mention of this in the plan may lose confidence in the ability of the entrepreneur. An example of a potential problem is over-dependence on a small number of customers. This is a common situation for small food manufacturers that sell to the large retail multiples.

Figure 3.11: Liquidity, Working Capital and Gearing Ratios

- **Current Ratio**: This compares the liquid (turned into cash within twelve months) assets with the liabilities due in the same period. A ratio in excess of 1 should be acceptable.

$$\frac{\text{Current Assets}}{\text{Current Liabilities}}$$

- **Acid Test Ratio**: This assess whether the business has sufficient liquid resources to meet its current liabilities.

$$\frac{\text{Current Assets — Stock}}{\text{Current Liabilities}}$$

- **Interest Cover**: This should indicate whether the venture has enough earnings to pay its interest costs after tax and interest. An interest cover of 2 times or less would be low and in excess of 3 times would be considered acceptable.

$$\frac{\text{Profit before Interest \& Tax}}{\text{Interest Charges}}$$

- **Turnover of Stock**: This indicates how long stock is held before it is sold. If the level of stock turnover is slowing down this may mean that stocks are piling up. Average Stock is opening stock plus closing stock divided by two.

$$\frac{\text{Cost of Sales}}{\text{Average Stock}}$$

- **Debtor Days**: This indicates how long it takes for debtors to pay.

$$\frac{\text{Sales X credit period}}{\text{No. of day in the period}}$$

- **Creditor Days**: This indicates how long the business takes before paying creditors.

$$\frac{\text{Creditors}}{\text{Credit Purchases}}$$

- **Capital Gearing**: A venture that is financed by a high level of borrowings is highly-geared. One with low levels of borrowings is lowly-geared. The level of gearing can have an impact on the amount of capital that the business can raise in the future.

$$\frac{\text{Preference shares + long term loans}}{\text{All shareholder's funds + long term loans}} \quad X \quad 100$$

Start-up Schedule
In this section, the entrepreneur should outline the timing of the start-up. Key events are prototype development, securing funding, locating premises, hiring staff, making the first sale, receiving the first customer cheque, etc. The entrepreneur may include a flow chart of these events. Failure to manage this schedule is a common problem for start-ups. Delays in starting can be very costly for a new business, as they usually mean increased expenditures and a longer time before revenues flow into the business.

Appendices
The appendices of the plan usually contain back-up material that is not necessary to the main text of the document, including items such as letters of intent from distributors, customers, suppliers and sub-contractors. Documentation gathered from primary and secondary sources used to support the plans may also be included.

CONCLUSION

At this stage, the entrepreneur has put in place the necessary funding for the new venture. The entrepreneur may be tempted to put aside the plan once the finance has been obtained and the venture launched. If this happens, the entrepreneur will have lost out on many of the benefits of the planning process.

The plan should be used by the entrepreneur as a guide to the company's day-to-day operations. The entrepreneur can enhance the effective implementation of the plan by putting in place monitoring and control procedures that can be used to assess progress on an on-going basis. Key control elements that should be monitored closely are sales, costs, inventory and quality. Corrective action should be taken if there are major deviations from the plan and the budgets. The plan should be updated on regular basis as the conditions change.

QUESTIONS

1. Outline the essential information that should be contained in a business plan?

2. Write a report for an entrepreneur outlining the content of the marketing section of the business plan. How does the marketing plan impact on the finance plan?

3. Identify the information required to prepare a business plan for a new business which will supply a cheese product to the retail multiples. Where would you source this information?

4. Use the STEP and Porter models to analyse one of the following industries:

   - The 3G mobile telecom market in Ireland
   - The tourism industry
   - Paper manufacturing
   - Recruitment industry

5. Choose a local industry and carry out a Competitor Profile of the leading competitors.

6. An investor has asked you to analyse the accounts of the Riverside Café Business Plan (Chapter 4). Write a report for the investor and make a recommendation on whether the Riverside Café is a good investment opportunity. (Use the ratios in Table 3.5 and Table 3.7 where appropriate.)

7. Prepare a Start-up Schedule for a new service business.

8. In a group, identify a business opportunity and prepare a business plan to raise the necessary capital from a financial institution.

REFERENCES

Porter, M. (1985): *Competitive Advantage*, New York: Free Press.

FURTHER READING

Ambrosini, G with Johnson, G and K. Scholes (1998): *Exploring Techniques of Analysis and Evaluation in Strategic Management*, Prentice Hall.

Duncan, R. (1972): 'Characteristics of organisational environments and perceived environmental uncertainty.' *Administrative Science Quarterly*, Vol. No. 3, pp.313-27.

Peger, R and Huff, A. (1993): 'Strategic groups: A cognitive perspective', *Strategic Management Journal*, Vol. 14 No.2, pp.103-24.

Schwartz, P. (1991): *The Art of the Long View*, London: Century Business.

4

RIVERSIDE CAFÉ BUSINESS PLAN[7]

EXECUTIVE SUMMARY

I am seeking a loan of €10,000 to set up a café in Ballydermot. Ballydermot is a provincial town where there has been major industrial development and tourism. Improvements in leisure facilities, particularly golfing, fishing and water sport, are attracting an increasing amount of tourists to the area each year. The restaurant will be specifically targeted at these segments.

The provision of wholesome and nutritious food will give the café an advantage over its two competitors, who have been concentrating on the fast food market, a market that is remaining static. They have failed to exploit a new market segment where there is a potential market of approximately 600 people. These customers will come from the following five customer segments: Management & Staff of Sierra Plastics, Visitors/Tourists, Self-employed, Gunne's Cement and Gravel Factory and Members of the Defence Forces. Potential customers showed a positive attitude towards the provision of a new style of café. There are high levels of dissatisfaction with existing facilities among locals in the town. Results of a survey show that 54% will use the café "frequently" and 38% will use it "occasionally".

Market research suggests that customers consider "quality of food", "price" and "variety" to be the most important attributes of a café. Therefore, this venture will concentrate on these factors. The café plans to capture 30 to 35% of the potential market in the first year and to grow its market share by five% in each of the subsequent years. The venture's pricing policy is based on industry averages and customer expectations.

The management function will be carried out by the principal of the venture, Deirdre Daly. The business will employ a fully qualified chef on a part-time basis and one full-time waitress. All sourcing of raw materials will be done locally.

---

[7] The authors acknowledge the contribution of Geraldine Loughlin to this chapter.

The financial figures attached are based on a €10,000 loan over five years at a rate of 10% interest. This money is required to purchase initial equipment and fittings and as working capital for the first year of business. Projected net profits are €2,000 in year one, €804 in year two and €1,975 in year three. Net cash flow for the first year is estimated at €2,980.

I am convinced that this business will be successful and profitable and that your loan will be repaid fully. I look forward to discussing this proposal with you.

Yours sincerely,
Deirdre Daly

1. DESCRIPTION OF THE BUSINESS

The café will be targeted at people working in the area and visitors and tourists to the town. Riverside Café will be open Monday to Saturday from 10 a.m. to 7 p.m. During the tourist season, it will open on Sunday afternoons from 2 p.m. to 7 p.m. The café will provide dinners, sandwiches, soups, salads, beverages (see Appendix 1). The café will concentrate on wholesome and nutritious food. This will differentiate Riverside Café from its competitors, both of whom concentrate on fast food.

2. THE BUSINESS ENVIRONMENT

The proposed location for the venture is Ballydermot. Ballydermot has been chosen for a number of important reasons:

- The town has undergone significant changes and developments in the last 10 years. The development of the Bloomfield Hotel, which is set in 300 acres including 50 acres of lakes and gardens, has attracted increased tourist trade to the area. The surrounding area is renowned for is championship golf course, fishing and boating activities on the River Gowan.
- The location of the US company Sierra Plastics in the town two years ago has increased employment in the town. Population figures have increased dramatically over the past few years and are predicted to rise further in the foreseeable future.
- The town has formed a committee aimed at improving the tourist trade in the area. Tourism figures for the region as a whole have been increasing in recent years by about eight percent per annum. Of particular importance are weekend breaks by Irish people.

- The town is located near the border and there is significant cross-border trade.
- I have lived in the town all my life. My family are well-known and respected in the area. I have built up a number of valuable business contacts that can be used.

3. MARKET RESEARCH AND ANALYSIS

Market Research

I conducted a survey to get the views and responses of potential customers. The questionnaire (Appendix 2) was targeted at a representative group of 50 people from all sectors of employment in the area. The most obvious and striking conclusion was that the town is severely lacking this type of service. The results of the questionnaire (Appendix 3) show that while 65% of people brought lunch with them to work, 54% said they would use a café in the town "frequently". A further 38% said they would use it "occasionally". The majority of potential customers considered that "quality of food" and "prices" would be the most important criteria when deciding when to use the proposed café. The main priorities of the café are:

- *Fresh produce and food*: This will be sourced daily from the highest quality local suppliers.
- *"Reasonable" prices*: The majority for those surveyed were prepared to pay €2 to €4 per day.
- *Variety*: The menu will offer variety in food and beverages.
- *Fast and friendly service.*

Market Segments

The market has been segmented based by occupation. The main occupational groups in the area are:

Students	Farmers	Managers
Professionals	Clerical	House Wives/Husbands
Construction Workers	Technical	Unemployed
Proprietors	Officials	Crafts people
Operators/Assistant		

Potential customers have been grouped into five categories:

- *Sierra Plastics*: Potential target market of 220 people. Sierra Plastics is a US company that located in the town two years ago.

Additional factory space is planned over the next two years with between 50 and 75 new jobs resulting.

- *Gunne's Cement and Gravel Factory*: Potential target market of 125 people. This company extracts and distributes building materials all over Ireland. It has been located in the town for the last 30 years. The owner-manager is supportive of local initiative.
- *The Defence Forces and Gardaí*: Potential target market of 155 people. While these personnel are based outside the town, they do account for a significant passing trade in the town.
- *Visitors/Tourists*: Potential target market of 90 people. These will include people staying at the Bloomfield Hotel. Some of the guests spend time visiting the town and its historic sites. Those people coming to the town to participate in leisure activities, such as fishing, golfing and water sports, may use the café. The completion of the new canal has meant that there will be a further increase in the number of visitors to the area in future years.
- *Local Business People*: Potential target market of 70 people. This segment includes those working in local public houses, newsagents, local professionals and the self-employed.

Market Size
From market research undertaken, the total market size is:

Sierra Plastics	220
Visitors/ Tourist	90
Professional & Self Employed	70
Gunne's Quarries	125
Defence Forces & Gardaí	155
Total Number of People	660

3.1 Projected Sales Volumes and Revenues 1998–2001

	Sales People*	Sales (per week)		Sales PA (per annum)
2002/03	130	€7.00	€910	€47,320
2003/04	135	€7.00	€945	€49,140
2004/05	140	€7.50	€1,050	€54,600

* *These estimates are based on research undertaken with customers (Appendix 2).*

> ** *The forecast is based on an average of €3.00 spend per visit. From the survey undertaken, 54% indicated they would use this service frequently and 38% indicated that they would use it occasionally during the week. Therefore it is estimated that the customers will use the restaurant on average 2 days per week.*

4. COMPETITORS

There are two competitors in the surrounding area. Information about competitors was obtained from secondary data, visiting their premises, personal experiences and hearsay.

Dec's Diner

This family owned business was established in 1987.
Strengths:

- It has a prime location in the town centre with good parking facilities.
- Due to its 10 years in business, it has built up a good reputation with customers.
- Their main business is in fast food but, in recent years, they have provided sandwiches, salads, tea/coffee which will be direct competition with the new venture.
- From the limited evidence that has been gathered, they appear to be financially stable and profitable.
- They have a 39% market share. They are the main competition in the area.

Weaknesses:

- They concentrate on the social trade: people who visit the "take-away" on their way home from the pubs or night-clubs.
- While a segment of their business will be in direct competition with the venture (the sandwiches and lunches) Riverside Café is focused on the lunch time market.
- This outlet doesn't advertise or promote its business and has the attitude that "we don't have to attract customers, they come in of their own accord". The management know that they have a dominant market share and believe that no other competition can or will take it from them.

Fosters' Take-Away

This family-owned business was established in 1975. Their business focuses on the sale of fast food to all segments of the market, with the majority of their customers being young people between the age of 18-30 years.

Strengths:

- Long-established business and the family owners are well acquainted with the people in the area.
- Have 25% of the existing market.
- A good location in the centre that is convenient to schools, pubs and night-clubs.
- Later opening hours at weekends and week-nights.
- Sponsor the local underage GAA teams.

Weaknesses:

- The market research rated them poor on "quality" and "variety". They received a "friendly service" rating of fair.
- In recent years, they have started to prepare dinners due to their continuing loss of market share. This is at odds with their existing reputation and image of being a "fast food joint".

Riverside Café will be competing to gain market share from these two competitors. However direct competition will be on a relatively small scale. Both of these outlets cater for the socialising and youth market and they stay open until 2.00 or 3.00 a.m. on Friday and Saturday nights. There is no doubt that the competition has some distinctive competencies in their business. However, the market research survey (Appendix 3) found that a lot of the people were dissatisfied with the level of service provided by the two competitors. Respondents rated "quality of service" and "price" as the most important factors in their purchasing decision. Both outlets were rated poor on "quality" but very good on "price". The focus of Riverside Café is to attract different segments of the market that have different needs. This will avoid direct competition with the existing outlets.

The common belief among the competition is that they are the only ones in the market and can divide the market between them. This is evident by their limited advertising and promotion. It was evident from the questionnaire that they have failed to recognise the increasing employment sector whose needs are not being adequately satisfied. This is where the Riverside Café will target successfully.

5. MARKETING PLAN

Market Strategy

Riverside Café's selling proposition is to capture the hearts and minds of the customer by providing high quality food, a variety of choice, affordable prices and a friendly and efficient service. The trend in recent years is that people are becoming more concerned about their diet and health. Therefore, Riverside Café will exploit this trend by only serving fresh, healthy and, where possible, locally-produced foods. The name of the venture, Riverside Café, suggests freshness and reflects what the business is attempting to achieve. As already outlined, the venture will be targeting the people who are working in Ballydermot and the surrounding areas and, on a smaller scale, visitors and tourists to the town. Based on the market research with these groups, it is clear that there is a need for this type of outlet and better quality food. The sector being targeted has grown steadily over the past five years and this trend is expected to continue into the future.

Pricing Policy

The pricing policy that the venture will pursue will be based on the following two factors:

- The prices customers are prepared to pay. From the market research undertaken 73% of those surveyed were prepared to pay between €2 and €4 per day (amounts went from a high of €5 to a low of 75c).

- Prices will be in line with industry norms.

Advertising, Promotion and PR

An extensive advertising campaign will be conducted one month before opening Riverside Café. Various media will be used to inform the target market about the café. A leaflet (Appendix 4) will be distributed to local factories, offices and shops. Advertisements will be placed in the two local newspapers, the "Ballydermot Evening News" and "Midland People". Free meals will be provided to local radio stations to be used as prizes in fun competitions. A local celebrity will be asked to open the restaurant. I will run a feature advertisement in the local papers to mark the opening.

Advertising will be concentrated in the first year of opening and particularly in the first few months. In subsequent years, advertising will consist mainly of promotions during festival and holiday times and the sponsorship of local events. In particular, sports events in the factories will be sponsored. The café will be offered as a location for prize-giving ceremonies.

Customer Service

A happy customer is worth more then spending on advertising. Customer satisfaction will be a priority at Riverside Café. I will seek feedback from customers to enable me to improve our service. In order to assess customer satisfaction, the business will put comment cards on each table (Appendix 5). This will have a direct impact on our operations. Where customers display dissatisfaction, the policy will be to give the customer a free meal.

6. MANAGEMENT TEAM & STAFFING REQUIREMENT

Management

This will be performed by Deirdre Daly, the principal of the business (Appendix 6). This will involve ensuring that the staff are performing the duties assigned to them, ordering from suppliers, stock taking and generally performing the daily duties involved in operating a café. I will also be preparing the accounts as I have relevant experience in this area.

Staffing

The venture will employ a part-time Chef to work from 9 a.m. to 2 p.m. His/her duties will include preparing the food for the day and writing the menus. Total hours worked will be 30 per week. A full-time waitress will also be employed. Duties will be taking and preparing customer orders, cleaning tables, etc. He/she will work 48 hours per week. A part-time waitress will be employed in the second year of operations if sales levels are achieved. These staff are available locally according to the local employment agencies. To achieve the planned service and quality levels, careful consideration will be given to the recruitment and selection of suitable staff. The qualities that will be required are:

- Capability to perform the tasks
- Ability to work in a small team environment
- Pleasant manner
- Clean appearance
- Commitment, motivation and honesty.

7. LOCATION AND OPERATIONS PLAN

Location

At present, there is a premises vacant on the main street in Ballydermot that would be suitable for Riverside Café. I have already had discussions with the owner. She is committed to converting the premises into a restaurant. The total area of the premises is 1,200 square feet. It was previously used as a bakery and therefore needs only minor alterations. The alterations include new seating, modernising the decor and some adjustments to the shop front and signage. I have agreed to renovate the premises and, if the business ceases trading in that location, an independent valuer will be brought in to put a price on my renovations and the owner will reimburse me. The owner is prepared to rent the premises for €10.00 per square foot per annum, payable in monthly instalments.

The layout plan for Riverside Café is shown in Appendix 7. On entering the premises, the sandwich and salad bar will be on the right to serve those wanting a take-away lunch. Down from there will be the hot food bar. Customers will serve themselves. The kitchen is perfect for use as it stands.

Equipment

The premises includes some equipment from the previous owners. The owner has agreed to sell this equipment to me. The cost of equipment will be:

Second-hand equipment:	Ovens	€4,000
	Cash Registers	€800
	Other Equipment	€500
		€5,300
New equipment:	Dishwasher	€600
	Fridge	€1,000
	Fixtures & Fittings	€900
		€2,500

Suppliers

The business intends to source each raw material from a single source. The aim of this is to build a lasting long-term buyer/supplier relationship. It is intended to draw up a contract with each supplier before beginning business and to negotiate all terms and conditions to ensure that both parties are satisfied with the arrangements. All of the raw materials will be sourced locally to ensure freshness and to build up credibility in the local community. The suppliers have been chosen based on the following criteria: quality of ingredients; delivery times and reliability; credit terms; and cost. The raw materials will be sourced from the following businesses, which I have already contacted.

Product	Supplier
Salads, Fruit & Vegetables	Western Fruit Ltd
Fish Red, Cold & White Meats	Harte Bros.
Salad Dressing, Cream, Milk,	
Cheese, Yoghurt, Butter	Farmers Co-op
Bread & Cakes	Quinn's Bakery
Other	Smith's Cash & Carry

Regulations

There are a number of pieces of legislation that the business must comply with, as it will be operating in the catering business. These are the Food Hygiene Regulations 1950-1989. Article 25 is the most relevant for the venture as it deals with the operation of a café (for example equipment, ventilation, temperatures).

8. FINANCE PLAN

See Appendix 8 for notes to the following accounts.

8.1: Projected Monthly Cash flow for 2002/03

Period	May	June	July	August	Sept.	Oct.	Nov.	Dec.	Jan.	Feb.	March	Apr.	Total
	€	€	€	€	€	€	€	€	€	€	€	€	€
Receipts													
Cash	3,943	3,943	3,943	3,943	3,943	3,943	3,943	3,943	3,943	3,943	3,943	3,947	47,320
Bank Loan	10,000												10,000
Total Receipts	13,943	3,943	3,943	3,943	3,943	3,943	3,943	3,943	3,943	3,943	3,943	3,947	57,320
Payments													
Cash Purchases	789	789	789	789	789	789	789	789	789	789	789	785	9,464
Rent & Rates	1,000	1,000	1,000	1,000	1,000	1,000	1,000	1,000	1,000	1,000	1,000	1,000	12,000
Light/Heat/Power						700						700	1,400
Repairs & Maintenance			125			125			125			125	500
Loan Repayments						1,000						1,000	2,000
Loan Interest			250			250			250			250	1,000
Insurance	250						250						500
Wages & Salaries	1,430	1,430	1,430	1,430	1,430	1,430	1,430	1,430	1,430	1,430	1,430	1,430	17,160
Legal & Professional Fees		208						208					416
Stationery & Telephone		100		100		100		100		100		100	600
Advertising & Promotion		600	350	100	100	100	50	50	50		50	50	1,500
Capital Expenditure	7,800												7,800
Total Payments	11,269	4,127	3,944	3,419	3,319	5,494	3,519	3,577	3,644	3,319	3,269	5,440	54,340
Net Cash flow	2,674	-184	-1	524	624	-1551	424	366	299	624	674	-1,493	2,980
Open Bank Balance		2,674	2,490	2,489	3,013	3,637	2,086	2,510	2,876	3,175	3,799	4,473	
Closing Bank Balance	2,674	2,490	2,489	3,013	3,637	2,086	2,510	2,876	3,175	3,799	4,473	2,980	2,980

8.2 Projected Cash flow at April 30th 2003, 2004, 2005

	Notes	2003	2004	2005
		€	€	€
Receipts				
Sales		47,320	49,140	54,600
Bank Loan		10,000		
TOTAL RECEIPTS		57,320	49,140	54,600
Payments				
Cash Purchases	1	9,464	9,828	10,920
Wages & Salaries	2	17,160	19,656	22,823
Rent & Rates	3	12,000	12,000	12,000
Heat, Light & Power	4	1,400	1,450	1,500
Repairs & Maintenance		500	500	500
Loan Repayment		2,000	2,000	2,000
Interest on Loan		1,000	1,000	1,000
Insurance		500	550	550
Legal & Professional Fees		416	400	410
Stationary & Telephone		600	750	790
Advertising & Promotion		1,500	1,500	1,500
Capital Expenditure		7,800		
TOTAL PAYMENTS		54,340	49,634	53,993
NET CASH FLOW		2,980	(494)	607
Opening Bank Balance		------	2,980	2,486
Closing Bank Balance		2,980	2,486	3,093

8.3 Projected Profit & Loss Account as at April 30th

	Notes	2003	2004	2005
		€	€	€
Sales		47,320	49,140	54,600
Less Cost of Sales		9,464	9,828	10,920
GROSS PROFIT		37,856	39,312	43,680
Less Expenses				
Wages & Salaries	2	17,160	19,656	22,823
Rent & Rates		12,000	12,000	12,000
Heat, Light & Power		1,400	1,450	1,500
Repairs & Maintenance		500	500	500
Interest on Loan		1,000	1,000	1,000
Insurance	6	500	550	550
Legal & Professional Fees		416	400	410
Stationary & Telephone		600	750	790
Advertising & Promotion		1,500	1,500	1,500
Depreciation	7	780	702	632
Total Expenses		35,856	38,508	41,705
NET PROFIT		2,000	804	1,975

8.4 Projected Balance Sheet as at April 30th

	Notes	2003	2004	2005
		€	€	€
Fixed Assets (FA)				
Fixtures, Fittings & Equipment (NBV)	7	7,020	6,318	5,686
Current Assets (CA)				
Cash		2,980	2,486	3,093
Current Liabilities (CL)		--------	--------	--------
Working Capital (CA-CL)		2,980	2,486	3,093
Total Net Assets (FA+CA-CL)		10,000	8,804	8,779
Financed by				
Long Term Borrowings		8,000	6,000	4,000
Retained Earnings		2,000	2,804	4,779
		10,000	8,804	8,779

9. OVERALL START-UP SCHEDULE

Task	Timing
Prepare Business Plan (including Market Research)	February 2002
Get Bank approval for Loan	March
Find suitable location and premises	March
Draw up contract with Lessor	March
Undertake renovations	April
Source Raw Materials and all Supplies	April
Interview for Staff	April
Advertising campaign	April
Opening of Riverside Café	May 2002

10. CRITICAL RISKS AND PROBLEMS

There are a number of potential risks facing this business. These risks are not all avoidable and therefore the business has to minimise its exposure to these where possible:

- The market research may be incorrect. Market research cannot eliminate the uncertainty and risks of the business.

- The competition may react to the new venture. Reaction might be price cuts and/or by providing a similar service. A new competitor may enter the market following the success of Riverside Café.

- Difficulties in getting high quality raw materials.

- Failure to secure enough financing.

- The closure of a factory in the locality or a reduction in tourism could reduce business significantly.

11. CONSOLIDATION AND RENEWAL STRATEGY

There are a number of ways the business might grow and develop. These are:

- The premises where the business is located has a second level, which is not currently being used. If the business grows and develops as outlined, this could be renovated and seating capacity could be expanded.

- The opening of similar business in another town where there is a similar opportunity.

- If the business is not successful, the premises could be used for holding Catering Courses.

Appendix 1: Sample Menu

Riverside Café

Salad Counter	**Hot Counter**
Ham Slice	Vegetables (Choice of 3)
Tuna Portion	Soup
Cheese Portion	Quiche
Coleslaw	Roast Beef
Egg Mayonnaise	Haddock
Salad Bowl	Roast Chicken
	Farmhouse Grill
Fresh Sandwiches/Rolls	Rice Based Dishes

Confectionery	**Beverages**
Scones	Tea/Coffee
Riverside Buns	Decaffeinated Coffee
Ham/Sugar Doughnut	Hot Chocolate
Danish Pastry	Minerals - Small/Large
Cream Cakes	Milk - Small/Large
Apple Pie	Mineral Water
Cheesecake	

Appendix 2: Questionnaire

I am researching the possibility of locating a restaurant in Ballydermot to cater for the needs of those working and living in the area. I would appreciate it if you would complete this questionnaire and I assure you that your replies will be kept in the strictest of confidence.

1. Where do you normally get and have your lunch?

   A. At Home

   B. Restaurant In Town

   If at a restaurant, please rank the following factors 1-5 in how you consider them to be satisfied.

Quality of Food	1	2	3	4	5
Price of Food	1	2	3	4	5
Friendly Service	1	2	3	4	5
Fast Service	1	2	3	4	5
Variety on Offer	1	2	3	4	5

   (1= Excellent, 2 = Very Good, 3 = Good, 4 = Fair, 5 = Poor)

   C. Bring Lunch with You

   If you bring a lunch, would you be willing to purchase fresh sandwiches if they were available?   Yes _____   No_____

   D. In another town.

2. How long is your lunch break?

       30 Minutes   _____

       1 Hour   _____

       1–2 Hours   _____

       More   _____

3. If a new restaurant opened in town, how often would you be prepared to use it?

       Frequently   _____ (4–5 days)

       Occasionally _____ (1–3 days)

       Never   _____

4. What is the maximum amount you would be prepare to spend every day on lunch?

       €1.00–€2.00_____

       €2.00–€3.00_____

       €3.00–€4.00_____

       Over €4.00 _____

5. Rank the factors you consider to be appropriate in providing this service?

1. Quality of food	1	2	3	4	5
2. Price of food	1	2	3	4	5
3. Friendly service ambience	1	2	3	4	5
4. Fast service	1	2	3	4	5
5. Variety on offer	1	2	3	4	5

   (1= Excellent, 2 = Very Good, 3 = Good, 4 = Fair, 5 = Poor)

Any other comments that you would like to make:

_____

_____

_____

_____

_____

Thank you for your co-operation

Appendix 3: Results of Questionnaire

1. Where do you normally get and have your lunch?

    A. At Home   8 %

    B. Restaurant in Town   17%

        The factors below were ranked as follows:

Quality of Food	Poor
Price of Food	Very Good
Friendly Service	Fair
Fast Service	Excellent
Variety on Offer	Poor

    C. Bring Lunch with You   65%

    If you bring a lunch, would you will be willing to purchase fresh sandwiches if they were available?   Yes   52%   No   48%

    D. Go to another town   10%

2. How long is your lunch break ?

30 Minutes	9%
1 Hour	78%
1–2 Hours	6%
More	7%

3. If a new restaurant opened in town, would you be prepared to use it?

Frequently	54%	(4–5 days)
Occasionally	38%	(1–3 days)
Never	8%	

4. What is the maximum amount you would be prepared to spend every day on lunch?

€1.00–€2.00	18%
€2.00–€3.00	42%
€3.00–€4.00	31%
Over €4.00	9%

5. Rank the factors you consider to be appropriate in providing this service?

1. Quality of food   32%
2. Price of food   29%
3. Friendly service ambience   14%
4. Fast service   10%
5. Variety on offer   15%

(1= Excellent, 2 = Very Good, 3 = Good, 4 = Fair, 5 = Poor)

Appendix 4: Advertising and PR

<u>*Riverside Café*</u>

Fed up and bored with your lunch?
Well now you have the option with healthy options !!

I am opening my restaurant on
Riverside Café
Ballydermot
on 15 May 2002

Myself and my highly competent team of staff will guarantee you fresh food daily, variety, keen prices, a pleasant ambience and of course a friendly service to remember.

Opening Offer of a 25% Discount
Come in and see for yourself

For further details — contact **Deirdre**
Telephone 098 765 4321

Appendix 5: Customer Comment Card

<u>***Riverside Café***</u>
<u>Comment Card</u>

Customer satisfaction is our priority. By completing this card with your comments and rating, you will help us to provide you with the standards you deserve.

Date:_____   Time:_____

Comments: _____
_____
_____

Please mark in accordance with the following scale:
Excellent: 9–10   Fair: 4–5
Good: 6–8   Poor : 1–3

Marks out of 10
Food: Variety
            Temperature
            Taste
Service: Efficiency
            Friendliness
Hygiene: Food Service
            Dining Area
            Staff
Premises: Comfort
            Lighting
            Atmosphere
Value For Money

Appendix 6: Curriculum Vitae

Personal Details:
Name: Deirdre Daly
Address: The Square, Ballydermot.
Telephone: 098 123 4567
Date of Birth: 27-2-1970

Education:
College: College of Catering, Cathal Brugha Street, Dublin
          Finals: Distinction
          Second Year: Merit
          First Year: Pass
          Final Year Project: Fresh French Pastries

Secondary School: The Convent, Ballydermot.
          Leaving Certificate Results: 3 B2s, 1 C1,
          2 D2s
          Intermediate Certificate Results: 2 A1s,
          2 B2's, 2 C1s, 2 D2s

Employment Experience:
The Bullman Inn: Manager.
Responsibility for managing the Bullman Inn. This is a public house owned by a major UK brewery. Specific responsibility for accounts, staffing and stock control. During my two years here I was awarded "pub-manager" of the year.

Bloomfield House Hotel: Assistant Chef.
This involved working long hours in a kitchen that serviced the hotel dining room. Each week-end several large functions would be held in the hotel (up to 500 people eating at any one time).

Lobster Bar, Cape Cod, USA: Waitress, Cashier.
The Lobster Bar could seat 75 people. I started waiting tables. After several months, I was made responsible for scheduling the other waitresses and then I was made responsible for handling the cash. I held this job for a number of summers.

The Old Lounge: Waitress.

Leisure Interests:
My main leisure activity is hill walking and rock climbing. I have travelled to several European countries to walk and climb. I am an active member of my local climbing club. In college I was Chairperson of the Climbing & Hill walking club.

Referees:
Bill McGrath, Lecturer, Cathal Brugha St., Dublin.
Sarah Flynn, Manager, Bloomfield Hotel, Ballydermot.

Appendix 7: Layout of Restaurant

Pay Here	Hot & Cold Beverages	Self Service Meals	Trays	Kitchen Area

In

Out

Cutlery Napkins etc.

Seating Numbers

6	4	4	4	2
6	4	4	4	2
6	4	4	4	2
6	4	4	4	2
6	4	4	4	2

Sandwich/ Salad Bar

Pay Here

Appendix 8: Notes to the Financial Accounts

1. *Cost of Sales*
Based on industry average of 20%. Due to the perishable nature of stock, most purchases will be made daily. Terms are cash on delivery.

2. *Wages & Salaries*
Part-time Chef
5 hours X 6 days = 30 hours; €90 pw X 52 weeks = €4,680
Full-time Waitress
8 hours X 6 days = 48 hours; €90 pw X 52 weeks = €4,680
Manager's Wages
€150 pw X 52 weeks = €7,800

In 2003, chef wages increase to €100; waitress wages increase to €108; manager's wages increase to €170 — all per week.

3. *Rent & Rates*
Rent is €10 per square foot per annum. At 1,200 sq. feet, total is €12,000.

4. *Heat, Light & Power*
Estimate from the ESB based on size of premises and the nature of
the business.

5. *Bank Loan*
Local bank offered a loan based on the following terms: Repayable
over 5 years at 10% per annum (fixed). Repayment of principal is
€10,000/5 years which is €2,000 per annum. Interest is €10,000 X
10%, which is €1,000 per annum.

6. *Insurance*
Local insurance broker made this estimate. It includes public liability
insurance.

7. *Depreciation*
Depreciation charged at 10%

Fixed Assets	€
Ovens X 2 (second hand)	4,000
Dishwashers (new)	600
Cash Registers (second hand)	800
Fixtures(new)	1,000
Fridge (new)	900
Other (second hand)	500
	7,800

	2002	**2003**	**2004**
	€	€	€
Fixed Assets	7,800	7,020	6,318
Depreciation (at 10%)	780	702	632
Net Book Value	7,020	6,318	5,686

5

PERSPECTIVES ON PLANNING

INTRODUCTION

The previous chapters have outlined how to prepare a business plan. Do entrepreneurs plan? Why do they invest time and money in preparing plans? What are the benefits of planning? Why do some entrepreneurs not plan despite these benefits? In this chapter a number of entrepreneurs discuss business planning and offer their insights into the planning process in new and small businesses. Research evidence on the planning process is discussed and an alternative perspective on planning for new businesses is suggested.

ENTREPRENEURS DISCUSS PLANNING

Chris is the owner of a large manufacturing business in the Midlands. This business is well established and the main supplier in the Irish market. Chris has recently started exporting into the European markets.

Emma is the owner of a new cafe in Cork city centre. The business is in its first year of operation and Emma is working "all hours of the day" to make a success of it.

Sean is a fish farmer in the West of Ireland. The business has grown rapidly in the last four years. The business exports most of its products to the French market.

Paul and Ciaran manufacture speciality food sauces. Their products are produced from organic ingredients and are sold as premium products in delicatessens.

Elizabeth is considering starting up her own software company to write a software programme for accountants in the UK. She has recently left college and started preparing her business plan within the last few months.

Why Do Entrepreneurs Prepare Plans?
Chris: The Koran summaries this simply: ". . . if you do not know where you are going, any road will take you there . . .". The most ba-

sic reason why an entrepreneur should plan is that it provides a direction to his activity. Starting a business needs all your resources, skills and time. Once you have started, all your attention will be directed to solving day-to-day problems and crises. It is difficult to stay focused on your longer-term objectives in this sort of environment. When I started, we had a lot of manufacturing problems and my attention was diverted away from marketing and distribution. Customers were unhappy with the distributor and we lost a lot of goodwill with our final customers. It took us two years to recover from this experience. A more detailed business plan might have helped us avoid many of our manufacturing problems.

Paul: A major reason for planning is to raise funds. Planning allows the entrepreneur to estimate the resources that are needed. These include not only financial resources but also the human resources, machinery and plant. Having identified the resources needed, the entrepreneur can calculate the financial requirements of the business. A business plan is essential if the entrepreneur is to raise finance from a bank or from a State agency. We could not have secured grant aid without a business plan. Our plan allowed the bank and the government agencies to assess the risk attached to our venture. As such, the business plan is the most essential tool for external communication that we had at start-up. A clear description of how an organisation proposes to develop a business allows investors to decide whether the project is a worthwhile investment and what is the risk attached to it.

Elizabeth: To test the feasibility of the idea. A business plan requires the entrepreneur to justify the market potential of the business. The greatest uncertainty facing an entrepreneur is the market potential for the business. The entrepreneur needs to answer questions such as: Is there a market for this product? Why will customers buy my product/service? Who are my competitors? Planning allows the entrepreneur to evaluate competitors and develop a sustainable competitive advantage. Planning forces the entrepreneur to choose explicitly a strategy for entering the market.

Planning is particularly important to entrepreneurs operating in uncertain environments. For example, in the software business, failure to plan may result in a lot of time and money invested in developing a product that the market does not want. It will take me two years to develop the product. It is essential that I am sure that there is a market for it.

Chris: The entrepreneur needs to establish the financial feasibility of the business idea. Having established that there is a market for the product/service, the entrepreneur must estimate the costs of providing this product/service and establish if this can be done at a cost that ensures that he is rewarded for both the risk he is taking and the time that he will be investing in the business. The entrepreneur should examine the accounts of competitors to see whether they are making money in this market. If others have failed or are losing money, the entrepreneur must seriously question the attractiveness of the market.

Sean: In some businesses, the entrepreneur will need to test the technical feasibility of the business idea. Purchasing fish cages and putting them in the Atlantic Ocean is a complex and risky business. You must know what you are doing. The entrepreneur can use the planning process to test whether he has the technical skills to operate the business and to produce the product. This may involve the production of a prototype. The entrepreneur needs to establish that the product will work, that it is possible to produce it in the volumes necessary and that raw materials are readily available.

Paul: An entrepreneur needs to plan at the start-up stage, and on an on-going basis, to maintain control of operations during and post launch. During the launch of the business, the entrepreneur will be working very long hours to get "up and running". The pressures of making it all happen will mean that the entrepreneur will be continually "fire-fighting". The existence of a plan will help the business to stay on course during this period of chaos. By planning, it is possible to ensure that everybody knows what their job is to be and they also know how well they must perform. This allows a certain type of control to be imposed over the business that would not be possible without a plan.

Chris: Essentially planning is used for allocating resources, benchmarking current activities and goals against desired performance and the performance of competitors, as an aid to decision-making and as a communications device.

The main reasons entrepreneurs prepare plans are summarised in Figure 5.1.

Figure 5.1: Reasons for Planning

- To give strategic direction to the business — What is it I want to do?

- To raise funds — Who will invest in this business?

- To test the feasibility of the business — Is there a viable market for this product?

- To test the financial feasibility of the business idea — Can I make a profit?

- To test the technical feasibility of the business — Can I make the product/provide the service?

- To control the business as it develops — What performance do I expect? Am I achieving this?

- To allocate resources and time — What should I be doing? On what should I be spending money?

What Benefits Did You Get From Planning?

Elizabeth: The software business is very dynamic and there is a lot of uncertainty about market demand. Planning increased my understanding of the external environment that will impact on my business.

Paul: Planning ensures that the entrepreneur's attention is focused on those factors that will determine success. In the business plan, the entrepreneur will have set targets for sales volumes, production volumes, and a timetable for development. In our business, it was essential that we secured distribution outlets that would generate sufficient volume. The result of preparing a plan was that we spent less time on product development, an activity that we enjoyed and were comfortable doing, and more time on the road trying to secure distribution agreements. Our business plan provides us with a set of targets against which we can measure our performance.

Chris: The process of planning ensures that I consider alternatives which otherwise might be ignored. Initially, I grew by responding to opportunities and approaches I received from overseas customers. However I discovered that not all of these markets were as attractive and that the cost of entering an overseas market is high. Since these experiences, I now evaluate each market and have chosen different entry strategies for different markets.

Sean: The main benefit that I got from the business plan was that it helped me raise finance. The banks and the State agencies were not interested in my business idea unless I produced a business plan. At first, I was reluctant to prepare the plan. I know the business well through my 15 years of experience. However, I found that the plan was a very useful control tool for the business. We continually check performance against planned performance. The business plan forms the agenda of our yearly business review. The process of preparing the business plan was a significant benefit. It helped me focus on allocating financial resources and my time.

Figure 5.2. Benefits of Planning

- Planning should reduce uncertainty about the business and the market.

- Planning should highlight the factors that are critical to the success of the business.

- Planning should ensure that alternatives are developed and considered.

- Planning should assist in dealing with banks, State agencies and investors.

What Problems and Difficulties Did You Have When You Prepared Your Business Plan?

Paul: The main problem that we encountered was in gathering information about the business and the market. The most difficult information to get is reliable estimates of market demand. At first, we looked at Government statistics, but the information was too aggregated to allow us to reliably estimate the size of demand for speciality sauces. Then we tried to estimate the size of competitors' sales. Competitors guard figures on their turnover, making it difficult to get any reliable estimates of total market size. We were able to get information from the Companies Registration Office on turnover for some of our main competitors. If the product or service is new, the entrepreneur will quickly discover that there is no available data on potential demand. Market research can often be unreliable as people find it difficult to estimate their usage of a new product or service. Often the best strategy is to talk to potential buyers of the product and if possible to talk to your competitor's sales force.

Elizabeth: My biggest difficulty to date is that I am not familiar with preparing financial accounts. Most entrepreneurs have little experience of preparing financial projections. This is often the most off-putting part of the planning process. I have the technical skills to develop the product but I do not have the necessary business skills to write a business plan. I think I lack the business, marketing and, in particular, the financial skills necessary for the preparation of a business plan.

Sean: I thought that I didn't have the time to spend planning. It has been estimated that it takes between 200 and 400 hours to produce a business plan. I was very involved in trying to get the business started. This required meeting suppliers, potential customers, Government agencies, equipment manufacturers and financial investors. Some of the time I spent preparing the business plan might have been better spent actually dealing with these people.

Emma: At first, I didn't appreciate the benefits of planning. My business is essentially a "self-employment" type of venture. My focus was on getting the business started and not on delaying the process unnecessarily by planning.

Figure 5.3: Difficulties in Planning

- Getting reliable and useful information.
- Lack of skills and expertise. In particular, poor financial skills.
- Lack of time.
- Lack of understanding of the benefits of the planning process.

You Have Discussed The Benefits of Planning. Why is it that Many Entrepreneurs Don't Plan?

Chris: Some entrepreneurs develop the business slowly and as a result have no formal written business plan at the outset. The nature and scope of the new business may not be clearly defined at start-up. The nature of some products and service businesses are such that the entrepreneur learns as the business develops. Many self-employed people, such as trades people and professionals, understand the business and their main concern is to develop a customer base as quickly as possible. The issues are clear and don't need to be stated in a formal plan. An entrepreneur with a skill to sell, for example a management consultant, may want to keep his options open for as long as possible.

Emma: Some businesses are small and the entrepreneur may believe they have a good understanding of the business. Often the entrepreneur may know all potential customers personally from previous business dealings. These entrepreneurs might talk through their business propositions with potential customers and financiers. This creates a mutual understanding as to the direction and scope of the proposed business.

Elizabeth: For many entrepreneurs, planning is an unknown. They lack the experience and skills to prepare a plan so they avoid planning.

The reasons why many entrepreneurs don't prepare plans are outlined in Table 5.4.

Figure 5.4: Reasons Why Entrepreneurs Don't Plan

- The entrepreneur is very familiar with the business
- The entrepreneur wants to keep options and alternative open
- The business is too small
- Planning is an unknown and the entrepreneur doesn't have any experience of planning.

If an Entrepreneur Lacks the Skills Should He Pay a Professional to Write the Plan?
Chris: My experience is that much of the benefit of planning is actually preparing the plan yourself. If an outsider prepares the plan, the entrepreneur will be less familiar with the content and the plan will have less of an impact on the running of the business. I would recommend that entrepreneurs get assistance in preparing the financial section of the plan if they are having difficulty doing this themselves.

In Your Experience What Are the Limits of the Planning Process?
Elizabeth: One of my main concerns about planning is that my plan may quickly go out of date. Obviously there will be unforeseen events that will happen in the market, which could be due to technological progress, mergers and acquisitions. I see completing my initial busi-

ness plan as a first step in a planning process. The business plan will be followed by continuous planning and updating of the plan as circumstances change.

The uncertainty surrounding the future may have a negative impact on the plan but it may also have a favourable effect. Changing circumstances may mean new more attractive opportunities. Some entrepreneurs want to keep all their options open. Preparing a plan means that they have to commit to one course of action. My philosophy is to focus on the software opportunity that I have identified and to monitor other opportunities. I want to avoid spending my scarce resources on other opportunities and be sure to make a success of this one.

Chris: Many aspects of a business plan are dependent on the successful implementation of another part of the plan. In the early days, I found that market feedback was different from what I had anticipated in my business plan. This resulted in a change of distribution outlet and a change in my product mix. This has a series of knock-on effects, for example the new distribution outlets needed higher quality packaging and faster delivery. Change in one area of the business will result in large sections of the initial plan becoming useless.

Emma: Planning may not always be the best strategy for an entrepreneur. Entrepreneurs are opportunistic, they seize opportunities quickly. The process of preparing a plan may lead the entrepreneur to procrastinate, what is called "paralysis by analysis". The entrepreneur may seek increasingly detailed information about the product or market and try to produce a more refined and detailed plan. This increased analysis may be an excuse for not implementing the idea and taking the first step to creating the new business. The implementation of the plan is of far greater importance than the preparation of the plan. In my situation, I needed to secure a lease for a premises. Once I committed myself to this, everything else fell into place. In many cases, the act of planning is not correlated with the success of a business venture. Similarly, the absence of planning cannot be used as the sole explanation of business failure.

Sean: Due to day-to-day pressures, the entrepreneur cannot afford the time and effort needed to examine the long-term future of the business. There is no point in worrying about the future if the business can't survive in the short-term. However, I accept that it is important that the long-term future of the company is not forgotten.

Paul: Entrepreneurs are required to prepare written plans. In my situation, we had talked about all the major issues and had written down our objectives and plans in some areas of activities. However, we had not produced a complete and integrated written plan. The banks and State agencies required this. At the time ,we felt we got little benefit from the added effort required to produce the written plan.

Figure 5.5: Limitations of Planning

> - Entrepreneurs are opportunistic. Planning may result in the missed of opportunities.
> - Formal written plans are time-consuming and expensive to prepare.
> - Plans may become out-dated due to changes in the business environment.
> - Changes in one section of the plan may result in the complete plan losing its relevance.

RESEARCH ON PLANNING

Do Entrepreneurs Prepare Effective Plans?

Research by the Bank of Ireland[8] suggests that entrepreneurs do not in fact have a good understanding of the financial viability of their business prior to start-up. This research shows that the financial figures produced by entrepreneurs will vary significantly from the actual outcomes once they start trading. This study compared the actual financial performance of new businesses with the business plan that was produced prior to start-up (Table 5.6).

---

[8] Research carried out by the Bank of Ireland Enterprise Research Unit.

Figure 5.6: Sales, Costs and Profitability: Forecasts Compared to Actual

	Forecast	Actual
Sales	100%	50%
Gross profits as a percentage of sales	45%	34%
Overheads as a percentage of sales	51%	129%
Net profits as a percentage of sales	4%	— 75%
Debtor Days	80	170
Stock Days	87	193
Credit Days	30	195

Sales, Costs and Profits

In comparing actual sales with forecast sales, the Bank of Ireland research showed that, on average, entrepreneurs forecast sales that were twice the actual sales achieved as entrepreneurs were over-optimistic about their business ideas. Entrepreneurs were better able to forecast costs, with actual costs being about 33% more than forecast costs (however, these actual costs were based on sales revenues that were 100% less than forecast). The impact of over-estimating sales and under-estimating costs was that, rather than achieving profitability, most new businesses achieved losses during the first year of trading.

Working Capital Requirements

The research also examined the ability of entrepreneurs to actually forecast working capital requirements. Entrepreneurs typically expected to be paid faster than was actually the case. Their stock turnover (the number of days it takes to sell stock) was slower than expected. The consequence of lower sales and slower payments was that the entrepreneurs themselves became increasing slow in paying their creditors.

Capital Requirements

Entrepreneurs typically under-estimated the amount of funding required to get their business up and running. Actual investment in fixed assets was over 90% more than forecast. The consequence of this and the losses incurred during trading was that the entrepreneur needed more funds. These additional funds were typically in the form of debt, with bank debt typically being six times higher than forecast by the end of the first year's trading.

For those businesses that survived, actual bank debt was only marginally higher than forecast at the end of the first year. This large increase in the use of debt financing meant that the ratio of debt investment to equity investment was typically 100% rather than the forecast 50%. In those businesses that failed, the entrepreneur's ability to forecast sales, costs, profitability, fixed capital requirements and working capital requirements was worse than the average described above. In particular, businesses that failed had much higher costs than were actually forecast. Also, their working capital needs were much higher than forecast. They were worse at collecting payments from customers (waiting on average eight months for payment).

Causes of Business Failure

Research suggests two main causes of failure. The first is the inability of new businesses to control costs when sales are significantly less than forecast. The second is the much higher indebtedness of these businesses and their over-reliance on borrowings rather than on equity investment. However well-prepared plans are, they are no guarantee of success. A new business that has prepared a good business plan and has received adequate financial investment may fail due to external market changes or competitive moves that were not possible to forecast in advance.

Do Entrepreneurs Prepare Plans?

The banking sector and the academic literature espouse the importance of preparing a business plan to entrepreneurs. Research suggests that many entrepreneurs don't prepare plans and, more importantly, many successful entrepreneurs do not prepare a formal business plan.

Research on the fastest growing US companies suggests that most companies had no formal plans (Bhide, 1986). Research on fast growth firms in Ireland suggests that many high growth businesses have no formal plan (Table 5.7) (Kinsella et al., 1994). The absence of a formal written plan in many successful start-ups might suggest that the preparation of a formal written plan is unnecessary. In fact, some might argue that it is a waste of the entrepreneur's time to engage in the preparation of a business plan if it does not affect the success and growth of the business.

Figure 5.7: Planning in the Fastest Growing US Companies

	USA	Irish
No plan	41%	47%
Basic plan	26%	—
Financial projections for investors	5%	—
Full business plans	28%	53%

Lessons on Planning: A Study of Entrepreneurs in the Irish Software Industry[9]

This study interviewed both entrepreneurs and bank lending officers. These groups are often critical of each other. Typical complaints from entrepreneurs are that the banks don't understand their business, and that they are too bureaucratic and slow in making decisions. Entrepreneurs in the Irish software industry were interviewed because it was believed that they would engage in planning. The researcher also interviewed the lending offices for new business from the main banks. The research conclusion was that entrepreneurs often did not understand the requirements of the bank. Similarly, the banks often did not appreciate what was involved in setting up a business and undervalued the entrepreneur's commitment to planning.

The entrepreneurs claimed that they made their own plans aside from the requirements of the banks. Some entrepreneurs develop two sets of plans: those they submit to the bank and those against which their business operates. They use planning as a tool to monitor the environment and to watch for changes. Entrepreneurs claim that they develop their "real plans" separately and do not share them with the bank. Their real plans are their own genuine expectations for the business. One entrepreneur explained that his business was doing very well and was surpassing many of his own expectations. However, in order to satisfy the bank, he had to tone down considerably his "real" projections for the period in order that the bank would accept them as feasible proposals. Despite this toning down, his own plans were closer to the mark.

---

[9] This research was carried out by Kevin Dowdall, Masters of Business Studies student, in his thesis, "Have Banks and Entrepreneurs a Mutual Understanding of the Planning Process?" (University College Dublin, 1996).

Lessons on Planning for the Entrepreneur

- **Managing the Finances**: The first lesson for entrepreneurs is
  that managing money is a very small part of the business of the
  bank. The banks' main business is managing information. In this
  regard, banks need information about the proposed business
  venture on paper where it can be referenced again and again.
  When the bank is ready to forward a loan, the information
  provided will be used as part of the loan terms and agreements.
  This means that the entrepreneur needs to be fully familiar with
  the plan at all stages of the application process.

- **Over-optimistic Projections**: The second lesson is not to be over
  ambitious in your projections for sales, lead times and so on. If you
  make an unrealistic looking presentation to a bank, it will not be
  entertained for very long.

- **Ability to Repay and a Market Opportunity**: Banks are
  interested in how much money you want to borrow, what you want
  it for, how you intend to pay it back and how quickly you will pay
  it back. They also want proof that your market exists and is big
  enough to carry your business. The bank has but a passing
  interest in the product or how it works. Repayment and
  profitability are the key interests of the bank. Entrepreneurs are
  considered to be a serious risk by the banks and lending
  institutions in general.

- **Communicating the Business Plan**: The business plan is used
  to communicate the objectives and for the control of resources. It is
  very important that the bank understands what your proposals
  are. The clearer and easier a plan is to follow, the more likely it is
  to be well received by a bank representative. Brevity is the key to
  good communication — say it once and say it well. With regard to
  control, the plan should explain how the entrepreneur proposes to
  manage the venture and the level of experience the entrepreneur
  has in the area.

- **Building the Relationship with the Bank**: Banks have an
  experience advantage over small business as they have seen small
  businesses succeed and fail. They know when plans are viable and
  when they are not. They know when an individual will drive a
  business and when he will chase it. Entrepreneurs should get to
  know the bank representative, take advantage of his experience
  and use him as a consultant rather than as a burden. Most
  importantly, at all times, the bank representative must be kept

informed of the organisation's position with regard to finance and markets.

- **Banks' "Gut Feeling"**: The seventh lesson is that bank representatives will use the "gut feeling" rule when processing an application. It is in the entrepreneur's best interests therefore to gain the confidence of the bank representative and at the same time promote the business venture.

- **Personal Creditability**: Finally, when you have found the bank and bank representative that is the best for your needs, remember that the bank's loan pivots on the entrepreneur's personal credibility. The entrepreneur must establish a rapport with the bank representative if there is any hope of the relationship flourishing.

Lessons on Planning for the Banker

- **Patience and Understanding**: Banks must understand that the entrepreneurs presenting plans have a different way of thinking about business and planning. Entrepreneurs do not like to be constrained by the formal planning process; however, this does not mean that they are poor planners. That said, entrepreneurs often spend so much of their time developing a product to sell that they lose sight of the cost of producing it. Patience is required on the side of the banks. Even if it seems that a product is going nowhere and that nobody would ever want to buy it, it is still important that the bank should insist that the entrepreneur presents some hard financial data about the proposal before making a decision.

- **Informational Resources**: Banks should tell the entrepreneur the information they will need to assess the proposal and the process that is involved in the bank's examination of the proposal. This should help prevent the entrepreneur missing out on the bank's informational needs. Rather than attending several information-gathering meetings, if the entrepreneur knew from the outset that he needed to provide a certain kinds of information then that could be arranged immediately.

- **Entrepreneurs' Limited Resources**: Banks need to remember that small businesses have limited resources. They are always short on experience and time. Written plans are not always available and it is unlikely that entrepreneurs will present very detailed interim proposals.

- **Rigorous Analysis of Plans**: Banks need to be very cautious that entrepreneurs are not simply telling them what they want to hear. This may involve them moving away from the hard financial data to look behind the entrepreneur. Whatever the bank chooses to do, simple financial analysis may soon become less important.

A NEW PERSPECTIVE ON PLANNING IN NEW AND SMALL BUSINESSES

Planning in New and Small Businesses Compared to Large Businesses

Experts suggest that entrepreneurs need to prepare a formal written business plan. This approach to planning is based on models of planning in large companies. The research discussed above shows that many entrepreneurs don't prepare written business plans and of those that do, many are quite poor at it. There are many factors that make planning different in the small business context and make the formal planning model suggested by experts inappropriate for new and small businesses.

The Relative Availability of Resources

Big business can afford to allocate resources to dedicated accounting, planning and production departments as deemed necessary and to buy in external advice when needed. New and small businesses generally do not have the resources to purchase the same services. The result is that the entrepreneur or small business owner is compelled to do his own consultancy work, becoming responsible for the different functional areas.

The Impact of Environmental Changes

New and small businesses are very susceptible to small environmental changes. For example, the loss of one customer may cause a new business to fail. Big and established businesses normally have sufficient resources to allow them survive minor environmental disturbances.

The Impact of Competition

Many new and small businesses operate in industries with low barriers to entry. The implication of this tends to be a very competitive market place and severe price competition. In an effort to generate sales, many new businesses will sell below cost. Unless the new competitor can develop a sustainable competitive advantage, it too will be the victim of the entry of more low-priced competitors. Large competitors will often have developed a more sustainable competitive advantage, for example by branding their products, by achieving economies of scale, etc.

Breadth of Experience

In planning in a large organisation, a complete set of skills and experiences will exist. Entrepreneurs and small business owners may not always have the same breadth of functional experience. Even where small business owners do have industry experience, they may not have the necessary level of experience for managing a whole organisation from book-keeping and finances through to recruitment and selection.

Role of the CEO

In large organisations, one of the key roles of the CEO is to make strategic decisions concerning the growth of the organisation. In comparison, the entrepreneur and small business manager has responsibility for the functional management of the business. Normally, the entrepreneur will be involved in providing the service to the customer.

Time Focus

The entrepreneur tends to be concerned with the present and does not have the time to be strategising about the future. The small businessperson has so many duties to carry out that he cannot possibly devote a lot of time to consciously working through where the organisation is going to be in, say, five year's time. His main concern is in how the organisation is going to call in its debts and pay its bills by the end of the coming month. Small businesses tend to have a shorter and more functional emphasis to planning.

An Alternative to the Formal Planning Model

Process versus Plan

The absence of a formal written plan does not mean that there is no planning process. There is a mistaken assumption that planning is about the production of a business plan. In many new and small businesses, the entrepreneur plans the development of his business but he may not take the trouble to put this plan to paper. In a general sense, planning is a reflective activity that precedes the making of a decision. In some situations, this period of analysis might be written up in a formal process but, for many decisions, it is more sensible to implement the decision immediately and proceed to consider other decisions and problems.

Some new businesses start-up on an incremental or part-time basis. As a result, they may not have a formal written business plan at the outset. Instead, the entrepreneur will probably have talked through his business proposal with stakeholders (for example, customers, suppliers, bankers, staff) and will have reached a mutual understanding with these stakeholders as to how the business should operate.

Partial Solutions versus Complete Plan

Planning is a problem-solving tool for entrepreneurs. At start-up, the entrepreneur must solve a series of problems of a varied nature. Some problems relate to immediate issues while others will have longer-term implications. Entrepreneurs do not have the time to fully evaluate every option or to consider all issues at once. The preparation of a business plan assumes that all issues are known and can be addressed in advance. The reality of start-up is that many issues and problems emerge during the start-up period and it is difficult to anticipate all of these in advance.

Soft versus Hard Information

Another mistaken assumption about the preparation of a business plan is that it is based on hard and detailed facts. However, this sort of detailed information is rarely available. In particular, when entrepreneurs are estimating the market potential of the business opportunity, they will seldom have access to the necessary market information. Entrepreneurs rely on "soft" forms of information. These include gossip, hearsay, and various other intangible scraps of information that the entrepreneur might get from individual customers, suppliers, competitors and friends. Often the quality of this information is superior to "hard data" of a more general nature. Entrepreneurs need not have complete and perfect information to prepare a plan and make decisions. The future of a business may be built on some information received from a small number of potential customers rather than a grand market survey. Often it can be difficult to prepare a written business plan based on this "soft" information.

Short Term versus Long Term

The nature of start-up is that the entrepreneur will focus attention on immediate issues and problems. Many of these decisions have long-term implications, for example, the choice of premises for a retail business. The entrepreneur must be conscious of the long-term strategic implications of short-term operational issues. The entrepreneur should ensure his daily activities lead towards the attainment of his long-term objectives.

CONCLUSION

In this chapter, we discussed the reality of preparing a business plan. There are many advantages to preparing a business plan both in terms of the final document and also the process of preparing the plan. However, research shows that many entrepreneurs don't prepare plans and that, of those that do, many are poor at planning. The biggest difficulty is preparing accurate and meaningful financial accounts. The chapter suggests that business planning is different from the "textbook" model. Entrepreneurs plan for the short term, focus on immediate issues and concerns and are motivated to solve problems.

QUESTIONS

1. Why should an entrepreneur write a business plan?
2. Research suggests that entrepreneurs are poor at planning. What are the difficulties that entrepreneurs encounter when writing a business plan?
3. How is planning in a small business different from planning in a large business?
4. Write the content of a speech that you would present to a group of bank managers that explains planning from the perspective of the entrepreneur.
5. Does the format of the business plan outlined in Chapters 2 and 3 reflect the reality of planning in new businesses?
6. Talk to an entrepreneur or small businessperson about their planning process.

REFERENCES

Bhide, A. (1986): "Hustle as Strategy", *Harvard Business Review*, September/October.

Kinsella, R. (1994): *Fast Growth Small Firms — An Irish Perspective*, Irish Management Institute: Dublin.

6

FINANCING THE ENTERPRISE

INTRODUCTION

One of the most important financial decisions at start-up is the raising and management of financial resources. The entrepreneur must put figures on the business idea. This will require an estimate of potential sales revenues and costs and of the amount of funding needed to start and operate the business. Funding is needed for purchasing fixed assets and to fund the working capital requirements of the business. Once the entrepreneur has identified the financial requirements of the new business it is necessary to raise the capital. The entrepreneur must then manage the capital and cash flow in the business. Poor cash flow management results in otherwise good ideas failing as businesses. This chapter examines the factors to consider when raising finance, the types of finance used by small businesses and sources of this finance.

RAISING FINANCE

Debt and Equity Finance

An entrepreneur may use a combination of debt and equity finance. Debt finance is money that the entrepreneur borrows. Equity finance is money invested in the business in return for a share in the ownership of the business. It is important that the entrepreneur balances the use of debt and equity.

The advantage of debt finance is that the entrepreneur retains control of the business. However, there is a risk attached to borrowing money, as the lender will usually have sought security for the loan. Failure to repay a loan may result in the new business failing. An over-reliance on debt finance is particularly risky for new businesses because of the lack of established cash flows. A further risk of debt finance is that increases in interest rates may require higher monthly loan repayments.

The advantage of equity finance is that there is no monthly cash outflow from the business. Equity investors are paid dividends from profits, only when the business can afford them. Equity investors in new businesses usually expect their ownership stake to increase in value because of the success of the business. This profit is realised when the equity investor sells the stake in the business. Many entrepreneurs find it difficult to attract outside equity investors and only have limited equity of their own to invest in their new business. Some entrepreneurs are slow to attract outside equity investors because they feel they may lose some control of their business.

Factors to Consider When Raising Finance

Nature of the Business

Not all businesses have the same capital requirements. A restaurant business will usually not need funding to test the feasibility of the idea. In contrast, a new bio-technology business may need funding to research and develop a prototype. A new manufacturing business may need funds to purchase machinery and stocks. In contrast, a new software company may not need capital to purchase much equipment but it will need extensive capital to fund the entrepreneur's time during the product development stage. Businesses that generate large cash flows will usually need less financing.

Stage of Business Development

The stage of development of the new business influences the level of risk of the investment. At an early stage, the new business needs capital that does not have to be repaid. An entrepreneur who needs to research a market and test the feasibility of a business idea does not want to borrow money to fund this expenditure. At this stage, the business has no revenues and will be unable to repay a loan. An entrepreneur or a business with a trading history will be more attractive to an investor because it has demonstrated that there is a market for the product/service.

Control and Ownership

Is the entrepreneur prepared to sell an equity stake in the business? This will mean that the entrepreneur is accountable to the investor. It may mean sharing managerial control. Most entrepreneurs find it difficult to offer equity to outside investors. The entrepreneur often delays selling equity in the belief that, as the business grows and develops, the price that will be received for the equity will increase. However, the lack of finance in the interim may impede the growth and development of the business.

Time

What will the finance be used for? If the finance is to fund long-term needs such as fixed assets or working capital, it is essential that long-term sources of finance are used. Many new and small businesses find it difficult to raise medium and long-term finance because of the high risk attached to the investments.

Exit Strategy

In raising finance, it is essential that the entrepreneur develops a way for the investors to "exit" from the investment. How will the investor get the capital and any profit out of the business? Most investors will want to "cash-in" their investment after a period of time. One of the easiest methods is to bring the venture to the stock market. This provides the initial investors with the choice of holding onto their investment for further capital gains or of selling their shares on the stock market.

Problems When Raising Finance

The entrepreneur faces a number of problems when trying to raise finance. These are:

- **Lack of Collateral**: The new venture has no assets or trading history against which an investor can evaluate the risk of the investment. Banks traditionally sought personal guarantees from entrepreneurs for loans. This practice has largely been discontinued by most banks in Ireland.

- **Lack of Accounting Expertise**: The entrepreneur may be inexperienced in preparing loan applications and *pro forma* accounts. The cost of an accountant and professional advice might seem quite high for the new business.

- **Identifying Sources**: The entrepreneur may be inexperienced in raising finance and may be unsure of where to seek it. There are a large number of agencies and bodies that assist new start-ups but the entrepreneur may find it difficult to identify the most appropriate source.

- **Interest Charges**: From the prospective of the bank, applications for small loans are relatively expensive to process. The same time and effort are needed to assess a €20,000 loan as a €200,000 loan, yet the profitability of the latter should be significantly higher. Banks charge a premium rate to entrepreneurs to compensate for the higher costs of processing loan applications and to cover the higher risk attached to a loan to a new business.

Approaching an Investor

The decision to seek venture capital is a difficult choice for an entrepreneur. As noted earlier, entrepreneurs tend to exhibit a strong desire for control and consequently they tend to be slow at involving "outsiders" in an ownership role. The reality is that, for many entrepreneurs, there is a need for outside capital. Entrepreneurs who are prepared to risk involving outsiders in an ownership role are often those that get the capital that grows the business. The process of raising venture capital can be time- and resource-consuming. The entrepreneur will have to prepare a plan and presentation for the venture capitalist.

There are a number of different factors that affect the decision of an investor to invest in a new or growing business. The important factors are:

- **People**. The investor is investing in the management potential of the entrepreneur, which is essential to the growth of the new venture. This can be more important than the business idea. The investor will examine the management record of the entrepreneur and the breadth of functional managerial skills required to run the business. The investor may insist that the entrepreneur hires marketing and finance professionals to enhance the management team capabilities. Many investors have a preference for an entrepreneurial team rather than an individual entrepreneur. In the US, it is considered reasonable to have started and failed a number of times before finally becoming successful. At the seed stage, the venture capitalist must make a decision based on the entrepreneur. Even if the idea has good potential, it cannot be realised without an entrepreneur with the appropriate skills.

- **Product/Service Idea**. The investor has to make a judgment on the future demand for the product/service. Where possible, the entrepreneur needs to demonstrate the product in operation. Investors are particularly pleased to see an existing customer base that have purchased and, where appropriate, re-purchased the product/service. If the business is at an early stage of development, the entrepreneur should have a working prototype of the product.

- **Magnitude of the Investment**. The investor will consider the fit between the proposal for funding and existing investment commitments. Many investors choose to specialise in certain sectors or in a certain stage of funding. Other investors may seek a spread of investments and may reject a proposal because they believe they are over-extended in a particular sector. Rejection from an investor does not mean that the proposal is flawed. Entrepreneurs often have to "knock on the doors" of many venture capitalists before they raise the finance.

THE "VALLEY OF DEATH"

The financing requirements of a new venture often do not peak at the start-up phase, as losses, slow sales and high costs inevitably create the need for more finance. Studies of the cumulative cash flow position of new businesses suggest that these cash deficits peak within two to three years of start-up. This cash requirement has been referred to as the "valley of death", also referred to as the "J-Curve" effect (Figure 6.1). It is during this time that most new businesses fail.

Figure 6.1: "J-Curve" — The "Valley of Death"

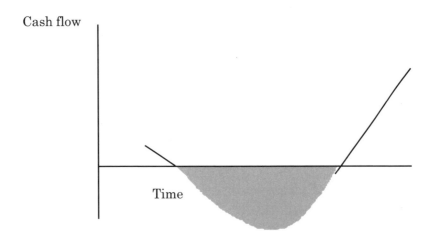

Cash flow

Time

There are a number of ways that the entrepreneur can seek to reduce this cash flow deficit:

- **Plan More Accurately**. The most difficult figure to estimate is sales. Entrepreneurs are often unsure of potential sales revenues and the timing of these revenues. Sales revenues, costs and capital requirements all need to be estimated more accurately. The ability to plan more accurately is increased with the entrepreneur's knowledge of the sector and previous experience of starting up a business.

- **Balance the Use of Equity and Loan Capital.** Too much reliance on loan capital increases the risk of failure. Loans must be repaid and incur a monthly interest charge. Equity investors expect to make their profit through capital gains and do not expect monthly repayments.

- **Reduce the Capital Expenditure of the Business.** This can be achieved by renting premises rather than buying them and by leasing equipment rather than purchasing it. There is a tendency of Irish companies to invest in premises and land rather than in more productive assets.

- **Cash Management.** Efficient cash management can increase new businesses chances of survival. Cash management involves ensuring that money owed is collected on time. This often does not happen because the entrepreneur is "busy" running the business. Some entrepreneurs are slow to pressurise customers for payment because they fear they might lose future sales. Cash management also ensures that expenditures are controlled and that the business takes advantage of discounts that are available.

TYPES OF FINANCE

There are three types of finance that a new venture may need: seed capital, venture capital, and development capital. Seed capital and venture capital are referred to as "early" stage financing, while development capital is referred to as "later" stage funding. To confuse matters further, sometimes all these three types of capital are referred to as "venture" capital.

Seed Capital

Seed capital is used to test the feasibility of a new business. This is usually required in manufacturing and high technology new ventures when there is a technological uncertainty concerning the product or process. This form of capital can be used to satisfy investors about the technical feasibility of the business opportunity. Seed capital may be used to fund the entrepreneur's time to develop a new product/process. In situations where there is a technical breakthrough, the entrepreneur may use some of the seed capital to file for patent protection.

Seed capital is the highest risk of all capital for new businesses. Therefore, it is inappropriate to borrow this type of finance. Seed capital is usually raised from family and friends and sometimes from private investors. The State agencies in Ireland award feasibility grants to some new businesses.

In making a seed capital investment, the investor must be aware of the high level of risk. The majority of seed capital is lost. The investor should investigate the entrepreneur and the process for developing and commercialising the new product/service. Sometimes, the inventor/developer is more interested in the technical performance of the product and will continually try to improve the product rather than bring it to the market. Also, if the inventor/developer is having difficulty, the investor should avoid being pulled into a cycle of investing more and more on the promise that this is the last amount needed to complete the feasibility testing.

Venture Capital

Venture capital is capital that is required to start-up the business. At this stage, there are more sources of finance available. This type of capital is used to purchase the assets of the business and to cover the initial operational losses that will be incurred. Working capital and operational losses are costs that many entrepreneurs fail to include when they are calculating their capital requirements. For some new ventures, start-up/venture capital will be required for up to the first five years of operation. There is a high risk attached to this capital, as the failure rate for new businesses in the first five years of operation is up to 60%. Venture capital companies that invest in start-ups lose significantly at this stage.

Research into Irish entrepreneurs has suggested that the principal source of start-up capital for new businesses in Ireland are bank loans and, where appropriate, government grants. This contrasts with the situation in the UK where entrepreneurs are much more likely to rely on their own personal savings. Possible reasons for the differences between Irish and UK entrepreneurs are first, the higher tax rates in Ireland make it difficult for Irish entrepreneurs to save and, second, the availability of government grants in Ireland. A recent survey by the Department of Enterprise and Employment showed that when raising equity most small firms rely heavily on private sources of finance (Table 6.1).

Figure 6.2: Sources of Equity Raised in the Small Firm Sector

Number of Employees	3-9	10-19	20-50	51-99	100+	All
	%	%	%	%	%	%
Private Sourcing	45	61	25	33	42	39
Business Expansion Scheme	38	22	43	38	29	36
Venture Capital	3	4	12	10	29	10
Other	14	13	20	19	0	15
	100	100	100	100	100	100

Development Capital

Development capital is used to finance the growth and expansion of the business. This capital is lower risk than both venture and seed capital because the business now has a trading record. Investors of development capital are particularly concerned with having an exit for their investment. The exit method that they prefer is the floating of the company on the stock exchange. Also included in "later" stage financing is replacement capital. This is money that is used to buy out the entrepreneur from the business and to fund management buy-outs.

SOURCES OF FINANCE

Raising finance can be a time-consuming and frustrating process for the entrepreneur. There are many sources of finance. The more important sources are listed below, however there are other sources that are available to particular businesses and in particular geographical areas. When raising finance, the entrepreneur may need to offer investors benefits beyond a straight cash return, for example one Irish hotel in financial difficulties offered an American customer of the hotel a free two-week holiday for the remainder of his life as part of an investment deal.

Sources of finance include:

- **Family and Friends**: This is a very common source of finance for small start-ups. It is a particularly good source of high risk capital. Problems may arise if there is not a formal legal contract between family members, however.

- **Bank Loans**: This is the most common source of finance for most small businesses. The advantage for the small business is that the entrepreneur can retain control and ownership of the business.

Over-reliance on debt finance may increase the financial risk of the business. Too much debt at the start-up stage may create a large cash outflow of interest repayments. Historically, it has been difficult for small businesses to raise long-term debt finance from banks. The banks prefer to lend for asset-backed loans and are slower to lend money for the working capital requirements of a business.

- **Government Agencies**: The most important of these agencies is Enterprise Ireland, which supports manufacturing and internationally traded services, for example financial services. Grants that are available include feasibility studies grants, employment grants, capital equipment grants, R&D grants, and grants for market development.

- **County Enterprise Boards**: County Enterprise Boards give grants for feasibility studies and for start-up. They tend to invest small amounts of money, as little as €1,270 for feasibility studies, with the average grants being about €13,000. The County Enterprise Boards have fewer restrictions but will only invest in businesses with less than 10 employees and where the financing need is less than €130,000. CEBs will not invest in start-ups that duplicate other existing businesses or are against public policy Also they operate at a local level and part of their brief is to encourage entrepreneurship.

- **Retained Earnings**: This is an important source of finance for many small businesses. Retained earnings are the profits of the business that are re-invested back into the business. The advantage of reinvesting profits is that the equity investment of the business increases without diluting the entrepreneur's control. Also tax is payable on dividends.

- **Government Tax Relief**: A number of tourist resorts, such as Ballybunion, Clonakilty and Tramore, have been designated as areas for renewal and are eligible for special tax breaks. Similarly, some urban and inner city areas have special tax exemptions, such as Temple Bar in Dublin and North Main Street in Cork.

- **Venture Capitalists**: They usually take an equity participation in a business. Most venture capital in Ireland is targeted at businesses at the development or growth stage. Increasingly, venture capital has become available for new start-ups, particularly in high technology sectors such as software. The venture capitalist will usually take an active involvement in the business in areas of financial management and strategic planning.

- **Private Investors**: These may be individuals who have made their own money in a different business and are interested in financing other entrepreneurs. This money is usually raised through personal contacts or through accountants.

- **Business Innovation Centres**: These have been set up with the assistance of the EU. The six in Ireland provide a wide range of services to people wanting to start their own business. They also provide information and access to sources of seed capital. They usually take an equity holding in the new venture.

- **European Union**: The Structural Funds that Ireland receives each year are disseminated through various operational programmes. Such programmes that may be of interest to small businesses are LEADER, INTERREG, and TELEMATIQUE.

- **Seed Capital Scheme**: This scheme allows entrepreneurs to claim three years of tax back if they start a business. Little use has been made of this scheme, due to its complicated structure and the fact that it is not well known.

- **Small Companies Market**: There has been increased use of the stock market as a source of finance for small companies. However, often these companies have approached the New York NASDAQ market to raise finance, for example computer companies Smartforce and IONA.

APPROACHING VENTURE CAPITALISTS

The process involved in raising venture capital finance has a number of clear stages (Table 6.2). First, the entrepreneur should establish that the venture capital is appropriate for the new venture. The entrepreneur needs to establish that the venture capitalist will consider investing in the particular industry and that the new business is at a stage of development that is appropriate to the venture capitalist. Having identified a number of potential sources of venture capital, the entrepreneur should submit a business plan.

A venture capitalist will read the proposal and either accept or reject it based on:

- Whether the area of investment is of interest
- The calibre of people involved
- Whether the accounts make sense and is it a solid investment.

In return for their investment, the venture capital firm will seek between 25 and 40% of the equity of the business. The venture capitalist will rarely invest in over 50% of the equity, as they want the management team to have a stake in ensuring the continued success of the business. The venture capitalist will seek a number of places on the board of the company to protect their investment. Venture capitalists will also seek a commitment from the entrepreneur that there is an exit mechanism. This will usually mean a commitment to bringing the company to the stock market within approximately five years of the initial investment.

Figure 6.3: Stages of Screening

Stage 1: Screening of Proposals
The venture capitalist will read the business proposal. Up to 80% of proposals will be screened out at this stage.

Stage 2: In-depth Examination
The remaining proposals will be examined in-depth. This will involve an analysis of the accounts, the product/service, and the market. The venture capitalist will have discussions with suppliers and customers of the proposed venture.

Stage 3: Meeting the Entrepreneur
If the venture capitalist is still interested, they will invite the entrepreneur and the management team to make a presentation of their proposal. This may involve a site visit to the business.

Stage 4: Due Diligence
If the venture capitalist makes a decision to invest, they will carry out a "due diligence" report, which is a complete audit of the business. The due diligence will check that the financial accounts are a true reflection of the state of the business. The venture capitalist will want to ensure that there are no hidden liabilities, such as outstanding actions against the company and that the company has full title to its assets. This may take between six to 12 weeks.

Venture capitalists seek a high capital appreciation on their investments. This is necessary because only a few of their investments are successful. The portfolio of a typical venture capitalist will have more businesses that will fail to reward the venture capitalist for the risk (Table 6.3) than those that are successful.

Figure 6.4: Venture Capitalist's Portfolio

20%	Companies successfully floated on the stock market.
40%	Companies are merged into a larger companies.
20%	"Living Dead" — companies that are surviving but haven't met the investors' expectations.
20%	Companies fail.

CONCLUSION

Cash is the lifeblood of new and small businesses. This chapter identified the crucial issues that an entrepreneur should consider when financing a new business idea. The challenge facing most entrepreneurs is to raise enough finance and to ensure that the appropriate type of finance is raised. Sources of finance for new and small businesses were outlined. Investors will use the finance plan to evaluate the business proposal.

QUESTIONS

1. What factors should an entrepreneur consider when raising finance?

2. What factors should an investor consider when investing in a new business idea?

3. It is often said that "cash is the lifeblood of a new business". How can an entrepreneur maximise the cash flow of the business?

4. A friend from college is considering starting a software business. Where might she get finance to fund the development of her new product idea?

5. Find out the criteria that a funding agency or investor in your area uses when investing in new or small businesses.

7

GROWTH STRATEGIES[10]

INTRODUCTION

Why do the majority of new start-ups stay very small or self-employment businesses, what are referred to as "micro-businesses"? Research evidence from the UK suggests that most new businesses do not achieve significant growth. This UK research showed that for every 100 new start-ups, only four will grow rapidly. In fact, 10 years after start-up, these fastest growing four businesses will account for half of all employment in those businesses that have survived. This chapter explores why only a small number of start-ups achieve growth. It outlines a model of the growth process and details the problems that the entrepreneur must "solve" at each stage.

Figure 7.1: The Case Of The Irish Graphics Display Industry

> *The Irish graphic display industry is highly fragmented, so much so that it is difficult to find agreement among participants as to what its boundaries actually are. There is a multitude of competitors, nearly all of which are small, owner-managed businesses. The market served is also highly varied and products are used by advertising agencies in corporate exhibitions, trade shows, in-store displays, visitor attractions, museums and heritage centres. Product "lines" (such as they are) are highly diverse, as each product will be tailored to suit customer needs. In the last two to three years, competition has become more intense as the industry growth rate has slowed and businesses have had to work harder to capture the business that does exist.*
>
> *The Irish industry is primarily Dublin-based. Marketing is primarily business-to-business and, in a small city like Dublin, personal contacts can be the key to attracting customers. Size is generally not an advantage when dealing with suppliers and buyers. In many cases, the small size of many of the businesses in the industry allows*

---

[10] The authors acknowledge the assistance of Aileen O'Toole in the preparation of this chapter. Her thesis is "The Growth Problems of Small Firms in the Irish Graphic Display Industry", Masters of Business Studies, 1996, University College Dublin.

them to serve customers more effectively, with a high level of flexibility, quick reaction times and a highly personalised service. The industry has a heavy creative content. Firms must first visualise their customers' needs and then turn them into something tangible. To do this, a personal service must be offered, as there will be a high degree of user-producer interface as the design and production process progresses. Entrepreneurs in small businesses in this industry were asked a number of questions.

Question 1: Is the ability and motivation of the owner-manager central to the success or failure of small businesses in this industry?

The entrepreneurs managed to avoid many of the mistakes made by small business owner-managers that are potential growth barriers, for example lack of managerial ability, unwillingness to delegate, a narrow product-market base. The entrepreneurs demonstrated high levels of motivation coupled with an element of realism about their shortcomings. This allowed them to seek help in areas where their skills were deficient. All have had little difficulty with delegation. Their ability to overcome the problems their businesses faced and to develop innovative solutions to problems appears to be one of the most important elements in their businesses' success to date.

Question 2: Is lack of finance a growth problem for small businesses in this industry?

No evidence was found to suggest that the availability of finance was a problem for the small businesses studied. The prevailing opinion amongst the entrepreneurs was that funding is usually available, providing the idea is good and it is presented effectively to the lender. Surprisingly, there was relatively little reliance on grants from the State agencies and, after their respective start-up periods, no grants were obtained.

Question 3: Are "labour legislation" and "red tape" barriers to growth for small businesses in this industry?

The costs of the benefits that must be provided to employees were criticised. However, they have not discouraged any of the entrepreneurs from hiring additional staff. Labour legislation was considered "inconvenient" rather than problematic. The legislative area that the entrepreneurs saw as providing the most significant problems for small businesses attempting to grow was taxation. The entrepreneurs claimed that punitive taxation prevents the re-investment of profits within the business and decreases the methods by which they can mo-

tivate their employees financially. The level of "red tape" was considered to be more of an inconvenience than a problem.

Conclusions

- *By far the biggest growth problem for small businesses in the Irish graphic display industry is the fragmented structure and limited markets of the industry itself. This may have forced the entrepreneurs of the businesses in the study to deviate from their core market niche into ancillary niches or sidelines in order to grow their businesses.*

- *The fact that lack of finance is no longer the serious growth problem it was once thought to be is something that public policy-makers have begun to recognise. Government should now turn its attention towards alleviating the tax burden on small businesses in an effort to promote further growth amongst small businesses within this industry.*

- *The findings emphasise the centrality of the entrepreneur to success in a small business. The dynamism and commitment of the entrepreneurs was obvious and their substantial abilities, coupled with their realism, accounted for their success.*

- *A significant growth problem that emerged in the cases (possibly related in some way to the level of "red tape" encountered) was the lack of time that entrepreneurs had to develop their businesses. This problem was especially severe before the first management layer was introduced but it was still an ongoing problem for the entrepreneurs.*

WHY DO SMALL BUSINESSES STAY SMALL?

External Barriers to Small Business Growth

These include:

- **Market Size**: Market size can be a serious barrier to growth for many small Irish companies. The size of the domestic market is limited by Ireland's small population. This means that small businesses must begin to export or operate in overseas markets when they are still quite small. Transport costs required to export may make a product/service uncompetitive.

- **Market Structure**: The structure of the market in which a small business operates may have a profound effect on its ability to grow. If the market is characterised by a standardised product, the

new business will be at a disadvantage relative to larger
businesses. If the market is characterised by many different
customer requirements, the small business may be able to grow
within a market niche.

- **Labour Costs and Labour Legislation**: High labour costs can
act as a deterrent for growth in small businesses. The cost of
labour increases with size, as more non-manual workers are
recruited who demand higher wages. In addition, the larger the
business gets, the greater the non-wage costs per employee as
employee facilities must be of a higher quality and benefits must
also be increased. Complying with labour legislation can create
additional costs that unfairly burden small businesses. Many of
the smallest businesses are exempt from such legislation, but
growth in employee numbers may mean that the legislation is
applicable. This may act as a de-motivating influence for
entrepreneurs contemplating growth.

- **"Red Tape"**: The level of paperwork required to operate even the
smallest of businesses places a heavy burden on the entrepreneur.
The Small Firms Association has estimated that a small business
faces an excessive burden of legal and regulatory issues in the
areas of tax (VAT, PAYE, PRSI) and industrial relations. Research
on fast-growth businesses in Ireland found that the major problem
experienced by Irish small businesses attempting to grow was the
time constraints on management. These entrepreneurs also
reported that government bureaucracy, the volume of paperwork
and the time it took to "get things done" was problematic.

Internal Barriers to Small Business Growth
These include:

- **Finance**: The ability to raise finance is a problem for new and
growing businesses. Small businesses face a number of difficulties
in raising finance. These are:

  ◊ *Low profitability*: Many small businesses have low profitability
  and find it difficult to generate internally the level of capital
  they require.

  ◊ *Level of funding*: The level of funding required for expansion
  can be very high when compared to the existing capital base of
  the business. This increases the bank's level of risk and
  consequently the banks seek a higher return on their
  investment.

◊ *Timing of funds*: The small business will require funds in lump sums rather than in small incremental amounts. For example, a food manufacturer wishing to increase capacity may have to acquire new premises, purchase new machinery and invest in the development of its market. These expenditures will be required before the benefits of the increased size will be experienced.

◊ *Competitive market structure*: Typically, small businesses are found in highly-fragmented industries such as wholesaling, retailing, services and job-shop manufacturing. These industries have low barriers to entry, making it easy for new competitors to enter the industry, increasing overall competition and lowering profitability. Competitors in these industries will often decrease prices to increase turnover but in the process they reduce overall profitability.

- **Narrow Product Base**: Most small businesses have a very narrow product range. The business may have been successful based on the entrepreneur's initial product/service. However, most entrepreneurs are slow to invest in product or market development.

- **Innovation**: The small business may not have the skills or resources to invest in product/service development and improvement. The initial business idea may have been innovative but, since start-up, the entrepreneur may have had to direct resources into managing the business on a day-to-day basis.

- **Poor Planning**: Most entrepreneurs are opportunistic when developing their businesses. Growth may require a more structured and formalised approach to market analysis. Most entrepreneurs do no strategic planning.

- **Quality of Staff**: The quality of the workforce in small businesses may also inhibit growth. Small businesses tend to start from a lower quality base in terms of employees. This may be due to the fact that the company may not be able to afford high quality staff, or because high quality staff may not be attracted to working in a small business with limited opportunities for advancement. In addition, the lack of resources available to train the existing work force, and thus increase its quality, may act as a growth barrier.

The Entrepreneur as a Barrier to Growth
The centrality of the entrepreneur in the small business is a powerful determinant of the future direction of the business. The very characteristics that are required to successfully start a small business can

work against the entrepreneur when the decision to grow the business is taken. The term "founder's disease" describes the failure of the founding entrepreneur to either adapt to the needs of a growing business or to leave the business.

The entrepreneur may retard the growth of the business for a number of reasons:

- **Desire to Retain Control**. Entrepreneurs seek to control the business. They may resist sharing control with others. This may prevent the entrepreneur hiring outside professionals or encouraging staff development and progression. The desire to maintain control may also reduce the capacity of the business to raise funds. Often entrepreneurs are unwilling to sell an equity stake in the business.

- **Poor Managerial Ability**. Most entrepreneurs and small businesses have very limited managerial skills. Often entrepreneurs have become successful because of their ability to create the product/service. Entrepreneurs frequently resent the increased formalisation that is associated with growth. A period of growth may highlight the entrepreneur's difficulties and weaknesses.

- **No Exit Strategy**. There may be barriers to the entrepreneur exiting from the business. A family business may lack a "heir apparent". Even if there is a suitable candidate within the family, many entrepreneurs are reluctant to pass on control. The business may not survive without the entrepreneur. It may be difficult to sell the business at a price that the entrepreneur considers acceptable.

In order to be successful, the owner-manager must not only have the will to grow but also, and perhaps more importantly, the skills necessary to manage the business. Changes in the attitude of the entrepreneur and the acquisition of new skills are almost always necessary if a business is to grow successfully. Some entrepreneurs cannot make the transition from being at the centre of a small business to being a manager of a large business.

A MODEL OF THE GROWTH PROCESS

Organisations don't grow of their own accord. Growth is the result of managerial decisions and actions. The growth of a small business can be described in terms of a number of common and identifiable stages (Figure 7.1). The transitions that occur as young, small and simple businesses become older, larger and more complex are similar in most small businesses. Most businesses appear to face similar problems at each of these stages. By understanding these stages, the entrepreneur should be able to anticipate the problems that will have to deal with in the future. A business may fail at any stage or may get "trapped" at a particular stage and progress no further.

Figure 7.2: A Model of the Growth Process

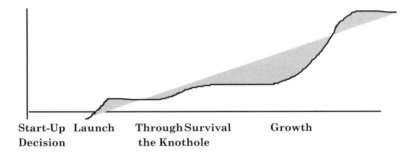

| Start-Up | Launch | Through | Survival | Growth |
| Decision | | the Knothole | | |

Start-up Decision

The most important decision the entrepreneur takes is to start the new business. It is normally an unconscious decision that happens over a long period of time. Experiences of family or friends in self-employment might sensitise the entrepreneur to the idea of starting a business. One of the most common characteristics among entrepreneurs is that a family member was involved in starting a business.

The personal creativity of the entrepreneur may be important. It may allow the entrepreneur to perceive opportunities where others see problems. The perception of a market opportunity may encourage the entrepreneur to start a business. This is referred to as being "pulled" into entrepreneurship. However many entrepreneurs are "pushed" into entrepreneurship. Circumstances such as losing a job, failing to get a promotion or frustration with the development of a business may "push" an entrepreneur to start-up. Crucial to the creation of a new business are the ambitions and personal characteristics of the entrepreneur. Support of family, spouses and friends may have an input into the decision.

The Start-up Decision stage may involve the development of a concept and the testing of its feasibility. The entrepreneur may develop a prototype of the product. The entrepreneur may begin to plan for start-up and may prepare a formal written business plan. In many businesses, the entrepreneur may have spent many years thinking about the product/service opportunity or on developing the product/service idea.

Launch

The most important activity during the launch stage is the acquisition of the resources necessary to get the business up and running. The entrepreneur will need resources such as premises, finance, and staff. Before the business is launched, the entrepreneur may need to sell the new idea to potential customers and investors. The business faces very high levels of uncertainty during this phase, for example, whether customers will buy the product, how often and at what price. During the launch phase, the entrepreneur is very dependent on outsiders. This is why personal contacts and experience in business are very important for entrepreneurs. The entrepreneur should focus on short-term activities that build the confidence of outsiders.

Initially, the business may be selling to "soft" customers. These are customers who buy the product or service because of a personal connection with the entrepreneur, for example a former employer or customers of a former employer. However these customers may not continue to use the business as it develops due to higher costs or lower quality relative to competitors.

This stage is characterised by an informal atmosphere. Staff will feel a strong sense of loyalty and mission, everybody will get involved in getting the business going.

Through the Knothole

Having survived the initial launch period, the new business must establish itself as a viable business concern. This period may be chaotic and stressful. The entrepreneur will have two main concerns at this stage. The first will be to establish a production process that is capable of producing the product/service in the quantities required. The second concern will be to develop the customer base of the business from the initial "soft" customers.

There will be a lot of learning by the entrepreneur during this phase. This learning will be about the business and what it will take to make it successful. The entrepreneurial activity that occurs during this period will play an important part in shaping the early development of the business. A strong sense of loyalty and mission will still exist among staff. Communications within the business will be very informal and will be free-flowing. A significant number of businesses fail during this stage. Estimates suggest that up to 30% of new businesses fail within three years of start-up.

Survival

Surviving the stressful "through the knothole" stage means that the business has established itself in the market-place. The focus of the entrepreneur's attention should now shift to the efficiency and profitability of the business. This may involve a review of costs, of the products produced and an assessment of the overall efficiency of the business. During this stage, the owner-manager will begin to formalise the organisation. Rules, systems and procedures may be introduced. The organisation and management style will become more conservative. The owner-manager may hire additional managerial or supervisory staff, for example a production manager. There will be a change in the attitudes of employees. They will no longer have the same sense of loyalty as was evident during the start-up and through the knothole stages. New staff will have been hired who where not part of the initial start-up. Increasing pressure for formalisation may lead to a decline in innovativeness. It is now necessary to protect the business that has been created. The majority of new businesses never progress beyond this stage. These businesses remain self-employment businesses for the entrepreneur.

Growth

This period of growth will only happen if the owner-manager chooses it (Figure 7.3).

The business has now established its distinctive competencies and has some product-market successes. To grow the business beyond the limitations of the existing niche will require acquiring resources in an attempt to realise the advantages that would result from larger scale. This may require the entrepreneur taking a risk that may be "larger" than the initial start-up risk, perhaps even "betting the whole business". It is essential that the entrepreneur has a good understanding of the future of the business.

This stage of growth is very management-intensive. The entrepreneur will probably play a less direct role in the day-to-day management of the business. New structures and procedures may be introduced. Internal informal "social" control may no longer be appropriate. Professional managers may have to be hired in all functional areas of the business. Finance is crucial if the business is to grow significantly. The entrepreneur will probably need to use the accumulated cash and the borrowing power that the company has established. It may be necessary for the entrepreneur to lose some control of the business by selling equity.

Businesses may continue to grow indefinitely or they may reach a plateau. Those that become medium-sized businesses are often referred to as "lifestyle" companies. They provide the owner-manager with the opportunity to withdraw from the day-to-day running of the business and to pursue other interests. Other businesses may be bought out and therefore may cease to grow as independent businesses. This is common in high technology businesses, for example small biotechnology companies get bought out by larger competitors if they are successful.

Figure 7.3: What Motivates an Entrepreneur to Grow a Business?

Growth may be sought for a number of reasons:

- **Survival and Stability**: Larger businesses have a lower failure rate. This may be due to their larger resources and their ability to influence the market they operate in. These larger resources allow the businesses to weather downturns in demand, short-term financial problems or mistakes by management. The same problems may bankrupt a smaller business.

- **"Status"**: The size of the business confers status on the entrepreneur. Size may be the benchmark used by external evaluators to judge the success of the business.

- **Scale**: Larger turnover allows the business to achieve lower costs and higher profits. Achieving economies of scale can result in significant savings in a small business.

- **Salaries**: Business growth may be pursued in order to obtain an increase in management salaries.

- **Adventure and Risk**: Why do entrepreneurs who have attained as much personal wealth as they desire continue to be aggressive in the marketplace? Entrepreneurs may grow their businesses because they like to take risks.

MANAGING A GROWTH BUSINESS

The model below can be used to highlight the problems that the entrepreneur will have to address and "solve" if the business is to grow (Table 7.2). The major strength of the model is that it is useful in gaining an understanding of the rather complex phenomenon of business growth and organisational development. However, different businesses will experience the stages and problems at different times. The problems and stages are a function of the age of the business, the size of the business and the business sector. Increases in the age and size of a business tend to be associated with increased organisational formality and conservatism. The sector in which the business operates will affect the business size required to support turnover, for example some businesses need complex organisation structures despite small numbers of staff while others may have large numbers of unskilled workers and relatively unsophisticated organisational structure.

Figure 7.4: Problems at Each Stage of the Growth Model

Stage		Problem
Start-up Decision	→	Commitment to "Going it alone"
Launch	→	Getting Resources Coping with Uncertainty
Through the Knot-hole	→	Producing the Product/Service Building a Customer Base
Survival	→	Marketing Expertise Limited Growth Opportunities
Growth	→	Managerial Skills Building an Organisation Finance

The problems and issues of each stage must be "solved" if the business is to grow. However, the factors that make a business successful at one stage of growth may not be applicable to the next stage, and may indeed cause the business to fail if a new set of skills is not learnt. This creates an enormous pressure for the entrepreneur. In the early stages of growth, the business depends on the entrepreneur's ability to make and sell the product. The operational abilities of the entrepreneur are most important at this time. The entrepreneur's ability to build and manage an organisation is not central to success. For example, the entrepreneur's ability to delegate is irrelevant as there are few, if any, employees to delegate to. As the business grows, the entrepreneur may have to develop new skills. The entrepreneur must spend less time "doing" and more time "managing". The organisation must become more sophisticated and complex in dealing with external changes, for example better internal and external information may be required, or better decision making styles may be needed. And, as a business grows, the administration challenge increases.

A survey of entrepreneurs of high-growth businesses in Ireland suggests that some entrepreneurs are better at managing the growth process (Table 7.4) (Kinsella & Mulvenna, 1993). "Fast growth firms" (FGF) were identified in terms of growth in profitability. Each FGF was compared to a similar or "matched" business. The matched businesses were in the same industry sector but had not experienced growth. Overall, the FGFs employed more than three times as many as the matched businesses.

Figure 7.5: Fast Growth Firms in Ireland

The study reached the following conclusions:

- FGFs were more aware of their market place, had a better understanding of their competitors, and kept in closer contact with their customers

- FGFs access a wider range of sources of finance at start-up and during growth than do the matched businesses. Grants are more important to FGFs

- FGFs believed that exporting would be very important to their future development. The matched businesses did not

- A higher proportion of FGFs were actively selling in export markets, making them less dependent on the domestic market

- FGFs had a larger share of the domestic market than did the matched businesses.

Managing rapid growth is about managing the transition from a personalised to an impersonalised leadership style and from a simple and informal organisation structure to a more formal organisation structure. A company experiencing rapid growth will face the following challenges (Hambrick & Crozier, 1985):

- **Instant Size**: This can create problems of disaffection, inadequate skills and inadequate systems.

- **A Sense of Infallibility**: This may result from the success of the strategies and plans employed by the organisation in order to bring about growth. Such organisations can become complacent in monitoring the environment for changes and new competitors.

- **Internal Turmoil**: This is created by the strain of growth. An influx of new people results in a staff that are not all that familiar with each other or with the company jockeying for position. Turf battles abound, decision-making suffers and people burnout or leave.

- **Extraordinary Resource Needs**: Often quickly growing businesses are cash-starved.

How can the entrepreneur best deal with these challenges? The key to successfully dealing with rapid growth is the ability to anticipate growth before it happens. An entrepreneur must ensure that the business has the resources and skills to handle growth in advance of actually needing them. Successful businesses avoid being lulled into a false sense of infallibility by using all available sources of information, even those that are unlikely to emit good news. They also develop processes for giving controversial data a fair airing. Successful businesses endeavour to halt a breakdown in decision-making that may result from the internal turmoil that the business is experiencing. This may be achieved by decentralising and using cross-functional decision-making teams. This also helps to assimilate new people and to speed up the decision-making process. Extraordinary resource needs may be coped with through the use of deferred compensation and stock options for workers and performance-related pay rather than fixed salaries.

Figure 7.6: Managing Rapid Growth: IONA Technologies

IONA Technologies was founded with a simple mission: to give organisations the freedom to integrate their computer systems quickly and easily (See Box 2.3 for background information). Its success has been built on making this mission a reality, based on core values and constantly reinforcing their simple but comprehensive vision of "Orbix Everywhere".

IONA has experienced rapid growth. As with any high-growth technology company, the strain of rapid growth has led to a number of challenges:

". . . lots of problems, technical problems, financial challenges and people issues. When you double the head count, half the staff have joined within the last 12 months, this leads to stress in the organisation" (Horn, 24/4/97).

Continued rapid growth placed a significant strain on IONA's management, operating procedures, financial resources, information systems, employees and facilities. The problems and challenges facing IONA are clearly of a strategic and organisational nature. The ability of IONA, and in particular the CEO Chris Horn, to build an organisation and professionalise the management team were essential to getting IONA to where it is today. The organisational and managerial problems facing IONA include:

- *Managing the transition from a small informal ad hoc organisation to a more structured and formal organisation*

- *Implementing systems and processes in the organisation*

- *Maintaining a culture that continues to innovate*

- *Motivating and managing "creative" employees*

- *Recruiting and retaining key staff*

- *Managing an organisation with multiple locations and senior management personnel in two locations (Ireland and US)*

- *Managing the rapid growth in the head count*

- *Attracting and integrating professional management ("grey-hair") into the organisation*

- *The necessity for Horn to change his management style. He appears to have successfully managed this transition. Even though he was one of the original three writers of the Orbix product, he now acts as CEO and not as a software developer*

> • *The issue of retaining senior and key personnel. Managing the organisation's dependence on these personnel and in particular on Chris Horn (founder, CEO and Chairman).*

CONCLUSION

Small businesses have common stages of growth and development. Achieving growth in a small business is a difficult challenge for the entrepreneur. Most small businesses remain small. This may be due to external market factors, to internal organisational weaknesses or due to the motivation and skills of the entrepreneur. Entrepreneurs who choose to grow their business must solve a number of difficult problems at each stage of growth. Essential to this growth process is the transformation of the business and the entrepreneur's ability to manage the business.

QUESTIONS

1. Discuss the internal and external barriers to small business growth.

2. In order for "a business to grow, the founder must go". Discuss.

3. Describe and discuss a model of the growth process. How might this model be useful to an entrepreneur?

4. What organisational challenges must an entrepreneur manage if a business is to achieve rapid growth?

5. Identify a business that has achieved rapid growth. Describe the growth and development of this business.

6. 'Is growth good for business.' Discuss.

REFERENCES

Hambrick, D. & L. Crozier (1985): "Stumblers and Stars in the Management of Rapid Growth", *Journal of Business Venturing*, Vol. 1.

Kinsella, R. & D. Mulvenna (1993): "Fast Growth Firms: Their Role in the Post-Culliton Industrial Strategy", *Administration,* 41(1), 3–15.

8

EXPORTING

INTRODUCTION

The small size of the Irish market means that many Irish companies must export to achieve growth. Also, in many technology and specialised businesses, the market in Ireland may be so small that the entrepreneur has to start exporting almost as soon as they start-up. In respect to exporting, the entrepreneur must make two key decisions. First, what are the appropriate export markets? Second, how best to generate sales in these markets, and how best to support customers? The basic choice is to sell directly to customers or to use an intermediate distributor or agent. There are many problems and difficulties for the new and small business that is trying to sell into overseas markets. This chapter examines these issues.

CHOOSING AN EXPORT MARKET STRATEGY

For a new business to succeed in its domestic and export markets, its product/service has to have some unique competitive advantage. A clear understanding of the target market and where the business' own product/service fits into the market is fundamental to success. Market knowledge is about understanding the market needs and translating these into products and services. The business should know how to approach the potential buyer, how often they purchase the product/service, what price they are prepared to pay, and what level of service they require. Sources of market information are to subscribe to trade magazines and e-mail discussion lists; to attend seminars and exhibitions; and to join professional organisations in the industry.

Figure 8.1: Largo Foods Goes International

Largo Foods manufactures over 60 different crisp product lines (Perri, Hunky Dory and own brand labels), has a turnover of more than €15 million, employs 200 people and exports between 40% and 45% of its output. In 1996, it secured cabinet space in 280 supermarkets across Britain for its additive-free Potato Cuisine brand. It has developed a good relationship with the UK multiples and supplies them with own brand crisps. The company sells other lines of crisps to markets such as the Lebanon, Singapore, Iceland, Dubai, Russia and Malta, where Perri is the brand leader. Largo also produces and supplies organic crisps to EuroDisney. Raymond Coyle, CEO of Largo, has a reputation for working the trade fairs, particularly the ISM in Cologne, which has enabled him to build an impressive contact-base. He works closely with the retail sector and is very responsive to their ideas. The motivation driving Largo's exports is the realisation that Tayto is the dominant player in the Irish market, with about 50% market-share — to survive, Largo had to export. The European market is not competitive, which made it easier for Largo to establish itself. However, competition on the home market has intensified with the entry of Walker Crisps from the UK, backed up by a high profile advertising campaign endorsed by Roy Keane.

To position a product/service effectively in an export market, there are three critical and interrelated questions that the entrepreneur must answer:

- **What niche will the business' product/service target and what margins are achievable?** Businesses must research new export markets before market entry. For a small business, the costs of new market entry are very high and failure in an overseas market may "bring down" the business. Research prior to market entry will ultimately save the business money. New and small businesses should focus financial and management resources into a niche market that is large enough to be profitable for the business but not large enough to attract the interest of larger competitors. Ideally, it should have worldwide potential. If a business attempts to sell to a broad target market, their message may not be heard by potential buyers. The difficulty for the entrepreneur is how best to define the niche market? Some businesses state that they are targeting a niche market, when in fact their focus is too broad. The benefits of finding a niche export market are:

◊ *Market Penetration*: The business should be able to identify potential buyers that match the target market criteria.

◊ *Low Levels of Competition*: This should make it easier to get established in the market and to gain market share.

◊ *Premium Prices*: It should be possible to charge customers a premium price.

◊ *Competitive Advantage*: The business should be able to build a sustainable competitive advantage based on the market knowledge that it develops.

The market research should not just be surveying or gathering of statistics. It should lead to a greater understanding of the market, of the buyers' expectations of the product/service, and of the structure of the distribution channels. A percentage of the product development budget should be set aside to investigate the market acceptability of the product/service.

- **What is the sales process and buying cycles in the target export market?** Once the new business has accurately defined its niche, the entrepreneur needs to research the buying processes operating in the target export market. This research should outline the stages involved from the initial inquiry to actual purchase. The business should seek ways of reducing the number of steps in the buying cycle in order to maximise their profit margin, since a long buying cycle would have a strong negative impact on cash flow. The buying cycle in the software industry is:

  ◊ Price of the software

  ◊ Product functionality

  ◊ Product technology

  ◊ Product development

  ◊ Upgrades

  ◊ Technical Support

  ◊ Training and implementation.

- **Who are the main competitors and what are their weaknesses?** The entrepreneur needs to identify the main competitors, their size, product range, financial capabilities, pricing policy, product functionality, customer support and use of distribution channels. A business with a strong focus strategy may appear to have no competitors in their niche, however other businesses may be covering the same market in a different way.

BUILDING THE CUSTOMER BASE

How Much Does It All Cost?

The general rule is that developing and exporting to foreign markets is expensive. It can be difficult for the business to secure sufficient funding when attempting to enter the overseas market. Existing overseas experience and existing overseas customers can help the business secure funding for new export markets. A comprehensive business plan can help raise funds. If the business seeks the financial support of third parties, it has to realise that this is a time-consuming process. The lead-in time for his could be as long as eight months.

Figure 8.2: Costs of Operating in Export Markets

• Travel and Subsistence.
• Meetings & Seminars.
• Telephone, Fax & E-mail.
• Sales Promotional Material Costs.
• Field Saleperson(s).
• Office Facilities;
• Discretionary Expenses (for example, meals and presents).

Direct or Indirect Channels of Market Delivery?

Given Ireland's geographical location, building a customer base in a foreign market can be a difficult and expensive task. The issues of market access will have fundamental implications on how the business will develop. Clearly, the existing elements of the classic marketing mix are important — product, price and promotion — but it is place that has added significance given the fact the business is exporting a product/service. The business needs to consider:

• How will the business generate sales in foreign markets?

• Will third parties be involved in generating sales leads and business development?

• Does the business need to establish a presence in the target markets?

- What customer support arrangements will the business make for its export customers?
- Should the company have offices in key markets?
- Can the business avail of or enter joint marketing and co-operation arrangements with other companies in the same industry when exporting products/services?

The business might choose to develop its customer base directly by setting up operations in export markets. Alternatively, the business might use third parties to represent itself in export markets. The entrepreneur will need to consider a number of factors in making this decision. Of particular importance is the type of customer support required, the pace of development the business is seeking and the resources of the business.

Figure 8.3: Factors Influencing the Choice of Direct or Indirect Exporting in the Software Industry

In case of the software industry, it is price and the value of a deal that governs the choice of distribution channels. The software business has limited raw materials and other inputs, therefore a trade-off has to be made between higher revenue from direct selling and a lower cost base from choosing the indirect route.

Influencing Factors	Choose Direct Channels	Choose Indirect Channels
Price	High	Low
Volume	Low	High
Software Complexity	High	Low
Buying Cycle	Long	Short
Support Requirements	High	Low
Other Service Element	High	Low

Direct Channels

A direct channel means that the business sells directly to customers in the export market. The business retains responsibility for every aspect of the sale from generating the initial sale to customer support. One of the main benefits of using direct channels is that the business retains control over all aspects of the sales and marketing of the product/service. However, one of the key assets that a business has to have in going direct to the market is a good sales team.

If the business is going the direct route, then a presence in the foreign target markets may be necessary for generating sales and for delivering customer support. A physical presence in a market is important for a number of reasons:

- Prospective clients want to see a tangible commitment and presence in the market
- Prospective clients can deal directly with the business
- Developing a new customer base can be done more easily in the target market.

There are other alternatives to setting up an office in an export market that give potential customers a point of contact. The most important factors for any business considering the options outlined below is that the easier it is for potential customers to contact the business, the greater the response rate is likely to be as a result. Alternatives to setting up offices in export markets include:

- **Remote Call Forwarding**: A potential customer dials a local number, which is automatically routed through to the business's Irish office.
- **Virtual Offices**: This is where the business has an arrangement that provides them with an address and telephone answering service in the export market.
- **Serviced Offices**: This is a similar set-up to the previous arrangement but includes shared secretarial support and some office space.
- **Staffed Field Office**: This involves some key personnel of the business establishing the field office in the export market and running the office in the initial stages. This is the most expensive option.

Generating Sales Leads Directly

The key decision for the business is to choose a method of sales generation that will deliver the greatest level of "lead" generation for the minimum capital outlay. Some of the methods that can be employed are as follows:

- **Direct Mail**: Direct mail is personal advertising sent directly to the potential customer. Direct mail should deliver pertinent information to a carefully selected group of individuals. If it fails to do this, it can be described as "junk" mail. Studies show that, on average, 80% of direct mail is opened and 63% is read. There are three critical elements that can enhance the direct mail process:

◊ *Use of a good "source list" of addresses*: When a business is choosing which external list to use, it has to consider the following: the origin of the names and the information, when the list was last updated and how often has the list been used by other companies

◊ *A good "offer"*: The business should emphasis the uniqueness of its product/service

◊ *Follow up on the lead*: The objective of the follow up may be to set up a meeting with the interested parties or to get feedback on the product/service.

- **Advertising**: Advertising in an export market should generate sales leads and should build the business's profile in the market. The objective of an advert is to generate enough interest that a potential customer will contact the business for further information about the product/service. If the business is going to advertise, the adverts should:

◊ Gain the attention of the target market and particularly the individuals who make the purchasing decisions

◊ Generate interest in the product/service

◊ Create the desire in the target market to buy the product

◊ Provide a way for the potential buyer to respond to the advert.

- **Trade Exhibitions and Showcases**: By participating in a trade exhibition, the business should meet with customers directly. Additionally, trade exhibitions should allow the business to assess competitors and to learn about future trends in the market. Sales generated at these types of events may be low unless the business has promoted it heavily before the actual event, through mailing, trade publications and magazines. The layout of the stand, product/service demonstrations, quality of the sales materials, the conduct and level of competence displayed by the business's representatives should constantly reinforce the unique selling point of the business. Trade exhibitions can be a relatively low cost way of meeting with buyers.

- **Promotion and Publicity**: In most markets, there are usually trade magazines dedicated to particular products/services. These publications are receptive to press releases, which can sell the benefits of the product but must contain some hard news as well. Other ways of promoting the product/service include speaking at trade conferences and writing articles in trade magazines.

Indirect Channels

Using indirect channels to enter or operate in an export market involves using the services of a third party, which can lower costs and speed up market entry. However, using a third party means a loss in control and less direct feedback from customers. The third party may not be as committed to selling the business's product/service as the business would be itself.

Alternative ways of generating sales and supporting customers indirectly are:

- **Agents**: These are businesses that sell the product/service on commission. Depending on the product/service the business is selling, it is often very difficult to find a suitable agent with the expertise and knowledge of the product and target market. In addition, there can be difficulty in getting an agent with the right mix of market contacts and entrepreneurial flair. Arrangements with agents usually take one of the following two forms:

    ◊ *Introducer*: In this case, the agent merely provides the initial sales lead and possible introductions to prospective buyers.

    ◊ *Sales Agent*: This is where the agent takes on the responsibility of identifying leads, demonstrating the product/service, dealing with further inquires and closing the deal. Consequently the commission that the agent receives under such an agreement is much higher.

- **Distributors**: A distributor doesn't make sales but just takes orders. It is up to the business in the target market to generate demand for the product. In most cases, the business will come to some form of arrangement with the distributor on joint co-operation with promotions and, where possible, may include the product in the distributor's catalogue.

- **Original Equipment Manufacturer (OEM)**: Depending on the nature of the product/service, the business could enter an agreement with an OEM manufacturer. This may mean bundling your product with the OEM's product. The margins in this type of arrangement tend to be low. The benefit is that there is minimal sales cost and the OEM can generate volumes of business that are far beyond what the business could achieve on its own.

Customer Support

Customer expectations for customer support have increased significantly in most industries. The business must establish the level of customer support that satisfies or exceeds customer requirements. The key for any business is to effectively exploit the potential of the customer relationship while, at the same time, minimising the cost of customer relationships.

If the business is going the direct channel route and directly supports customers, the decision has to be made whether to do it from an Irish base or from the target market base. Supporting customers from the Irish base may be seen as a disadvantage by foreign customers. However, if the business can demonstrate that it successfully supports other buyers from Ireland, this may become less of an issue.

Customer support can be a significant cost if it is not carefully managed. Where indirect channels are used, it is essential that a decision is made about who will provide customer support. If the business is using indirect channels, the business becomes removed from its customers and may lose out on customer feedback. Maintaining effective customer support is advantageous because it provides feedback. Customers can be used to test new ideas, to provide feedback on product performance, and to learn about competitors. Additionally, it may be possible to earn revenue by charging customers for service contracts or maintenance contracts.

CHOOSING A PARTNER

No matter what type of partnership the business enters into with a third party, it is essential that the business gets it right from the start. Entering an export market is an expensive process and will consume a lot of management time. Many companies get only one chance at entering a new market. The process that is involved in identifying and evaluating potential partners is as follows:

- Decide on what type of partnershipis most suitable for the business

- List all potential partner candidates

- Evaluate the potential partners. Partners should be compared using the following criteria: customer base; resources; market knowledge; sales and marketing skills; geographic scope; commitment

- Meet with the short-listed partners to discuss possible arrangements and verify that some form of "chemistry" exists
- Enter an arrangement for a trial period in order to sort out problems that arise
- After the trial period, enter a legal agreement.

Most small Irish businesses are not in a strong negotiating position to lay "down the law" when negotiating a partnershiparrangement. However, the deal should include the following points:

- Level of commission
- Target sales volume
- Staffing levels
- Promotional activities
- Penalties for non-achievement
- Opt out clauses
- Exclusivity of the arrangement.

The management of the distributor/agent is a key determinate of the success or failure of a business in an export market. The involvement of each party can be developed by:

- Allocating responsibilities and developing joint marketing activities
- Communicating regularly, thereby keeping abreast of latest developments
- Swapping market intelligence data in relation to new developments in the market
- Putting in place a formal process of meeting and regular reviews and targets
- Appointing persons in both businesses to be responsible for managing the partnershiprelationship.

EXPORT PROBLEMS

External Barriers
External barriers include:

- **Financial Problems**: These problems include currency devaluations and the high cost of capital in foreign markets. Any business that is exporting to a foreign market is at risk due to currency fluctuations and devaluation. The introduction of the Euro in 2002 has eased this problem in a European context.

- **Government Export Policy**: Government policy towards exporters and exporting is a crucial determinant of success. Government policy may ease a business's exporting problems or they may create additional problems due to high travel costs or poor infrastructure. Importantly for small businesses, governments may provide advice on how to enter foreign markets.

- **Overseas Competition**: The business may experience strong competition from competitors established in the foreign market. Many exporting businesses cite "competition" as a major obstacle to exporting.

- **Bureaucracy**: The preparation of documentation such as shipping documents, export licenses, bills of lading can be a very time-consuming process. This problem is more significant in small businesses due to a lack of management and financial resources.

- **"Red Tape" in Importing Countries**: Governments may block imports in a number of ways such as imposing tariffs and increasing custom inspections. Procedural barriers may arise due to cultural differences and differences in local regulations and requirements.

- **Delays in Payments**: There are significant delays in the length of time taken to make payments for products/services supplied to overseas markets. The delays can be due to poor documentation or slow payment by the purchaser. This impacts on an exporter's cash flow and financial position.

- **Export Documentation**: In theory, the advent of GATT and various EU agreements should have reduced the amount of paper that accompanies shipments. However, several empirical studies have concluded that delays in preparing complex export documentation still pose significant problems to exporters.

- **Logistical Constraints**: The problems of physically getting the product to an overseas market can add significantly to the cost of the product. Some governments have imposed restrictions on the use and type of heavy goods vehicles that can be used on their national routes at certain times of the week. This therefore impacts on the business's ability to deliver the product within certain time commitments.

Internal Problems
These include:

- **Inability to Finance Exports**: For some businesses, lending institutions perceive the risk of exporting as being too high, given the size of the actual business, the high cost of exporting, and the insufficient level of capital in the business. New businesses tend to underestimate the cost of exporting and the level of price competition in export markets.

- **Product Considerations**: The product/service may require significant adaptation before it can be sold into a foreign market. These problems can relate to packaging and labelling, quality and safety standards, and the establishment of a suitable design and image for the overseas markets.

- **Lack of International Marketing Expertise**: For an exporting drive to succeed, it is necessary to have top management commitment. Some problems may occur due to inefficient marketing strategies and low managerial commitment to the whole exporting process.

- **Difficulties in Sourcing Reputable Distributors**: A business may have difficulty in finding a reliable and capable distributor. In addition, this process can be compounded by the fact that the legal system may be "pro" distributor. This makes it extremely difficult to terminate the services of a distributor. To help overcome this difficulty, the business should use trade missions or personal visits to the target overseas market to gain the necessary information and contacts.

- **Lack of Information and Market Research**: Before a business considers entering a foreign market, it has to gather good quality information. However, sourcing this information often can be a problem due to the location of the market, a lack of expertise in collecting and collating market intelligence, and linguistic barriers.

- **Poor Communication with Foreign Customers**: Customer habits, languages and other cultural nuances have an impact on the way relationships with foreign customers are forged and maintained. Foreign cultures can be difficult to understand. Translating product attributes into foreign languages can present problems.

- **Lack of Promotion in Foreign Markets**: Overseas promotion can be problematic. The tendency among exporters is to standardise promotional practices rather than adapt them to local conditions. Empirical studies have shown that small businesses have greater problem in this regard because they have fewer resources to overcome communication problems.

CONCLUSION

This chapter has outlined the various steps that a business has to go through in order to minimise its own risks and to maximise its rewards in foreign markets. It is important to note that there are significant risks and uncertainties attached to exporting a product or service. A business has to plan its export strategies to reduce these risks and overcome the potential problems that were outlined in the chapter. Due to the limited size of the Irish market, it is imperative that firms look further afield to develop their customer base.

QUESTIONS

1. What factors should an entrepreneur consider when choosing an export market?
2. Discuss the implications of directly generating sales in export markets?
3. What are the indirect channels of building a customer base?
4. What criteria should an entrepreneur consider when seeking a partner in an export market?
5. What internal and external problems might a small business experience when exporting?
6. Develop an export strategy for a food product.

9

NETWORKS AND ALLIANCES

INTRODUCTION[11]

Economic theory argues that all businesses are profit-maximisers and that they compete with each other for scarce resources. However, in many cases, entrepreneurial businesses network or form alliances to compete against larger better-resourced businesses. Entrepreneurs who co-operate with other small businesses believe that their goals are positively linked. As one small business achieves its goals, so will other members of the network or alliance. These cooperative arrangements should result in the sharing of expertise and resources and to a reduction in costs.

The theme of this chapter is the nature of inter-firm collaborations and the role they can play in the development of SMEs. This chapter focuses on the different types of collaboration between businesses and the motives behind these collaborations. These include networks, alliances and supply chain relationships. The role of information technology in cooperative agreements is discussed.

NETWORKING

While entrepreneurs have their own independent businesses, most are involved in and operate within a network of one kind or another. Entrepreneurs spend over half of their time dealing with people outside of their own business. At the most basic level, an entrepreneur will rely extensively on an informal network of family, friends and other business people as well as the more formal network of banks, accountants and lawyers. Research suggests that more successful entrepreneurs are particularly active in networking with business people, regulators and union representatives. Indeed, the success of a small business often depends on informal person-to-person networks, word-of-mouth recommendations and repeat business based on suc-

---

[11] The authors acknowledge the contribution of this chapter by Paul O'Reilly, Department of Management Studies, Dublin Institute of Technology.

cessful earlier assignments or personal contacts acquired. "Networking" for the small business describes the relationship between the enterprise and its external environment. These relationships may take several forms:

- **Demand-Related Networks**: These networks involve dealings with customers, obtaining new business and the maintenance or establishment of contacts with customers.

- **Supply-Related Networks**: These networks involve the cooperative supply of a product or service.

- **Support Networks**: These networks include banks, business advisers, family and friends.

Network relationships are less structured than those in more formal strategic alliances and joint ventures. This lack of structure requires the entrepreneur to be more motivated and skilful in developing mutually rewarding, cooperative arrangements. Indeed, the entrepreneur must be persistent in developing the network support critical for the growth of the businesses.

Innovation Centres and Incubator Complexes

Incubator complexes are becoming increasingly popular for new enterprises. These centres provide a range of services to the new business. Of most importance is the provision of low cost office and production space. Other services include assistance in project evaluation, marketing, secretarial support, and advise on financing and bookkeeping. Management development is encouraged through the availability of business advisors, training and workshops. These centres can also play a key role in helping the enterprise access financial assistance. Intangible benefits for the entrepreneur is the network of entrepreneurs who may be experiencing similar problems and difficulties. Universities are popular locations for such complexes. Start-up companies are located at all the major universities and Institutes of Technology in Ireland. These companies can avail of educational and training programmes, computing facilities, access to research and expertise of staff in the college and other general services that are available on campus.

Figure 9.1: Industry Integration: The Irish Mushroom Sector

A swift and efficient supply chain has been a critical factor in the Irish mushroom industry becoming the largest per capita exporter of mushrooms in the world, with a growth rate of 33% per annum between 1990 and 1996.

Production has changed from on-farm compost manufacture and production in trays, to a satellite system where mushroom compost is manufactured centrally and production is in bags on satellite farms. Mushroom production is labour-intensive but the satellite system of production disperses labour requirements over a large number of holdings where family labour predominates. There are six compost manufacturers and over 550 mushroom farms. Growers are concentrated near marketing enterprises, which in some cases also double-up as marketing companies. Where this is the case, it is not uncommon to find the mushroom composter/exporter financing the grower's capital costs. Three large marketing companies account for most of the exports. The need to preserve freshness meant a concentration of marketing companies in locations that offer convenient access to cross-channel transport.

This shuttle-style operation and grower network offers many advantages and has been designed to ensure:

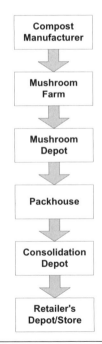

- *The central composter, by specialisation, can supply a compost material of the highest quality*

- *The grower network allows for flexibility to increase mushroom production as market conditions dictate, and the individual grower with relatively small units and personal incentive can give attention to detail*

- *The central marketing system guarantees maximum penetration of export markets and provides guarantees for continuity of supply of high quality product*

- *Specific growers can be used to selectively harvest mushrooms for individual customers to meet very strict specifications and packaging requirements*

- *The segregated grower network plays an important role in curtailing the spreading of disease in mushroom crops.*

Figure 9.2: Irish Seafood Producers Group

In 1986, Irish Seafood Producers Group was established by five salmon farmers, based in and around Connemara, County Galway, as a marketing and distribution company. Prior to the establishment of ISPG, these individual farmers competed against each other on the French market. Frequently, the outcome of this competition was that the farmers were "played-off" against each other by French wholesalers. This resulted in lower prices for all the suppliers. The objective of the alliance was to benefit the farmers in terms of economies of scale, improved bargaining power with customers and better access to the market. Additionally, it would provide a reliable delivery chain. Poor delivery by suppliers had in the past generated a very poor image of the Irish seafood industry in the Continental European marketplace.

Today, ISPG is the largest supplier of farmed salmon and trout operating in Ireland. It supplies product to the fresh and processing trades under the "Bia Mara" and "Donegal Silver" labels. Some 70% of ISPG's catch is exported to France, Spain, the UK, Germany and Switzerland. Currently, more than 15 people are employed directly by ISPG in Kilkiernan, Connemara, in addition to the 250-plus people working throughout the network of production and packing companies linked to ISPG. These include eight salmon farms, in locations stretching from Donegal to Cork.

The trading relationship is that the farms must supply all of their fish output to ISPG and ISPG must pay them at the week's market rate. The way the company operates is quite flexible, allowing the fish farms to link up with ISPG depending on the markets they wish to supply. ISPG meets with the farms to agree a schedule on when to take the stock. ISPG dictates what quantity of fish is required to be harvested to meet market demands.

Salmon and trout are supplied from the group's four packing plants located on the west coast of Ireland. Two of these plants are certified to ISO 9000 level and all operate a hazard analysis system, ensuring that the high standards of hygiene are in operation at all times. Product is supplied to the domestic market on the day after harvest, with product shipped to export markets to arrive within 48 hours of harvest.

Industrial Networking

Industrial networking is a form of co-operation involving a binding agreement between two or more companies for the purpose of sharing costs and strengthening expertise in such areas as research and development. Its aim is self-help and it is particularly suited to small and medium-sized enterprises that wish to develop and grow but are constrained by a lack of financial resources and technical expertise. A network group can be confined to a region, to a country or it can be trans-national. The degree of innovation and synergy achievable is in proportion to the commitment, respect and loyalty developed between the partners. To assist the strategic development of SMEs in Ireland, Enterprise Ireland has been promoting inter-firm co-operation networks. The objective of this initiative is to develop formal partnerships that will assist the development of small businesses.

HORIZONTAL ALLIANCES

A horizontal alliance is a collaboration between businesses operating at the same stage of the production process. Horizontal alliances emerged as a popular mode of operation in the 1970s when businesses began to realise that that they were unable to cope with the increasingly complex environment. Businesses that choose to follow a strategy of forming horizontal alliances seek to obtain materials, skills, know-how, finance, or access to markets through co-operation rather than through ownership.

Horizontal alliances between businesses may:

- Increase the bargaining strength of the businesses when they are dealings with major buyer/sellers

- Help the businesses penetrate markets and, in particular, export markets

- Reduce costs by sharing expenditure on research and development or market development.

Alliance partners may share upstream activities, such as the sourcing of raw materials; downstream activities, such as marketing and distribution; or operational activities, such as production. There are three basic types of strategic alliances possible between businesses (Chakravarthy & Lorange, 1991):

- **Type 1**: This type of strategic alliance seeks to combine the upstream strengths of one business with the downstream strengths of the prospective ally. The benefit of such an alliance is to gain insight and access to the partner's technological and manufacturing know-how or to benefit from the partner's established position in the marketplace.

- **Type 2**: This type combines the downstream activities of the two co-operating businesses. It may call for the merging of their product lines and sales/service channels. The alliance may be able to offer a broader product line and provide systematic solutions to the customers of both partners.

- **Type 3**: The third type of alliance combines the operational capabilities of the partners to exploit economies of scale. This type of alliance may also seek to combine the research and development capabilities of the partners, for example important complementary technologies may be made available to the co-operating businesses through such an alliance.

A horizontal alliance may take a variety of forms. The alliance may be limited to a specific project or may be of a more enduring and all encompassing nature. Alliances may either be a loose relationship, for example a network; a contractual relationship, for example subcontracting, licensing, franchising; or a formal integration, for example an acquisition or merger (Table 9.1).

Formation of a Horizontal Alliance

There are four stages to the formation of a horizontal alliance:

- **Ensure that the venture has the support of key stakeholders**: The partners get to know each other and clarify that they are mutually acceptable to one another. It is important that a good personal chemistry exists between entrepreneurs in both businesses and that the joint venture is seen in a positive light by all the participants.

- **Assess the strategic fit of the alliance**: An analysis of the strategic fit between the partners is necessary to ensure that both partners perceive the alliance to be a win/win situation.

- **Selling the alliance**: The co-operating businesses must ensure that all stakeholders "buy-in" to the alliance. Multiple points of contact between the co-operating businesses should be established.

- **Specify strategic plans and implementation responsibilities**: The partners should discuss how the alliance will be managed and controlled between them, including:
    - ◊ The exact ownership structure of the alliance

◊ The legal liabilities of the partners

◊ The staffing of the venture

◊ The physical location of the venture

◊ The financial obligations of the partners.

Figure 9.3: Types of Horizontal Alliances

Network: This is an arrangement whereby two or more organisations work together through a mechanism of mutual advantage and trust. There is no formal relationship between the parties.

Subcontracting: This involves a business subcontracting a particular service or part of a process.

Licensing: This is the purchase or sale by contract of a product or process technology, of a design or of marketing expertise. It is common in science-based industries, where, for example, the right to manufacture a patented product is granted for a fee.

Franchising: This is a form of marketing and distribution in which the franchiser grants an individual or small company, the franchisee, the right to do business in a prescribed manner over a certain period of time, in a specified place. Franchising has been the fastest-growing retailing form in recent years.

Consortia: A group of two or more independent organisations that agree to work together jointly on some undertaking, each contributing some particular resource or expertise.

Joint Venture: An arrangement whereby organisations remain independent but set up a newly-created organisation jointly-owned by the partners. Forms of joint venture include:

- *Spider's Web Strategy*: A joint venture with a larger competitor

- *Go-together then Split Strategy:* Companies co-operate over a fixed period and then separate. This is often used for specific projects

- *Successive Integration Strategy:* Starts with weak inter-firm linkages, develops towards interdependence and concludes with a take-over/merger.

There are a number of disadvantages to forming a strategic alliance. Firstly, a strategic alliance requires that the profits are shared if the new venture is a success. Secondly, when a business enters into an alliance, there is a risk that critical know-how will be lost to its alliance partner. The alliance partner might subsequently use this know-how to compete directly with the business. The third disadvantage of alliances is that the partners must share control. Conflicts over how to run the venture can destroy it as a viable business. This can be particularly difficult for entrepreneurs, given their desire for autonomy and independence.

MANAGING THE SUPPLY CHAIN: VERTICAL ALLIANCES

The Supply Chain

A key feature of most industries is that rarely will a single business undertake all the activities from raw material production through to marketing and supporting of the final consumer. Businesses will usually specialise on one part of this system. This system of activities is referred to as the value chain. To understand how value is created, it is not sufficient to look solely at an individual business. It is necessary to consider the other aspects of the value chain. In many industries, much of the value creation will occur in the supply and distribution chains and not at the manufacturing stage.

The linkages in the value system can be illustrated by considering the way a business's suppliers provide products/services that it uses in its value chain (Figure 9.1). The suppliers' value chains interact with the business' value chain in a number of ways, for example, when the business' procurement department interacts with the suppliers' order entry system. These linkages provide opportunities for the business to enhance its competitive positioning and for its suppliers to benefit as well. A business might accomplish this by influencing the configuration of its suppliers' value chains to jointly optimise the performance of certain activities and by improving the co-ordination between its value chain and its suppliers' value chains. The key point to take from this is that the company's relationship with its suppliers can be one in which both gain; one need not gain at the expense of the other. In the food industry, vertical partnerships between retailers, manufacturers, distributors and farmers are becoming increasingly common.

Figure 9.4: IKEA Redefines the Furniture Industry Value Chain

Traditionally, the value chain in the furniture industry was fragmented and customers tended to receive low levels of service and, in
many cases, poor product design. Delivery was difficult and expensive
and frustrating for the consumer. Retailing was concentrated in over-
crowded department stores, where products were presented poorly.
Transport costs for assemblers and the cost of holding stocks were
high. There were a large number of small part manufacturers and assemblers, who made to stock. The industry was characterised by low
design standards and high working capital requirements. The value
chain was:

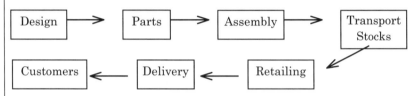

IKEA identified design and retailing as the key activities in the value
chain. Examining customer requirements showed there was demand
for a product with a high design content retailing at a moderate price.
IKEA designed these products to a "Scandinavian" image. Additional
value was created for customers by designing spacious stores, located
"out-of-town" to avoid high rents. Products were presented in ready-
made rooms so that customers could see how the product might look
in their own homes. Realising that consumers would be young married couples with children, these stores opened at week-ends and provided crèche facilities.

   IKEA sub-contracted manufacture of the parts. Assembly and
transport problems were "solved" by designing products to be "flat
packed", so customers would take the product home themselves and
assemble it. The "part" manufacturers were controlled using a sophisticated computerised stock control and ordering system.

   IKEA redesigned the value chain:

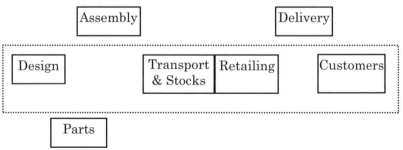

Figure 9.5: The Value System

SUPPLIER
VALUE CHAINS

CHANNEL
VALUE CHAINS

CUSTOMERS
VALUE CHAINS

ORGANISATION'S
VALUE CHAIN

SOURCE: PORTER 1985

Supply Chain Management
Supply chain management is a concept that has evolved in recent
years to reflect the fundamental changes that have occurred in the
relationship between the producers of primary products, manufacturers and retailers. Supply chain management is concerned with
the linkages in the supply chain, from primary producer to final consumer. A supply chain, in its full meaning, consists of a complex
network of links and nodes that engage in converting raw material
to consumption form and bringing the product to the customer. The
supply chain is traditionally divided into two distinct sub-chains: the
upstream chain, often referred to as materials management, which
links the manufacturer and his suppliers, and the downstream
chain, which links the manufacturer and the retailer and end-
consumer in a physical distribution sub-chain. Of the two sub-
chains, the upstream chain clearly leads in the development of close
co-operation among its constituent members. In practice, supply
chain management seeks to break down the barriers that exist between each of the links in the supply chain, in order to achieve
higher levels of service and substantial savings in costs.

The relationship between the supply chain partners was formerly adversarial in nature. Buyers sought to exert their influence and achieve lower costs. This was often achieved by getting suppliers to compete against each other and awarding contracts to the lowest price supplier. However companies such as Marks & Spencers and Toyota have shown that mutual gains can be achieved if purchasers co-operate with other members of the supply chain. In many industries, these adversarial relationships between supply chain partners and their suppliers are giving way to cooperative partnerships in which both try to improve the flow of product and information in the distribution channel system (Table 9.2). The idea is to create maximum value for the customer through vertical co-operation. A lasting supply chain partnership based on trust should enable a business to improve their profitability. Other benefits include improved price stability, better customer support, reduced transaction costs, increased innovation, and economies of scale.

Figure 9.6: Stages of Supply Management

Typically, there are four stages that describe the relationship between the customer and the supplier:

Stage 1: Confrontation with the supplier.

Stage 2: An arm's length relationship. Adversarial attitudes gradually give way to a cautious assessment of a working relationship.

Stage 3: A sharing of mutual goals.

Stage 4: A partnership between customers and suppliers.

Figure 9.7: Customer-Supplier Partnerships

The American Hospital Supply Corporation (AHS) provides on-line order entry terminals at hospitals for buyers of hospital supplies. AHS carries a very broad range of products. Hospital buyers can use the terminals to inquire about stock availability, price and delivery and then place an order. The success of this system has meant that AHS has been able to expand its product range to include office supplies and even medical supplies from competitors. This system has created a single interface for buyers to reach their many suppliers, who now reach new customers at lower costs. AHS has developed significant new revenues by offering a package of multi-vendor services.

Information Technology and Supply Chain Management
New management approaches and new information technologies are making it easier for companies to co-ordinate their activities. Information technology has played a critical role in the development of supply chain partnerships and the management of vertical linkages in the value system. Information systems crossing company lines are now quite common and, in some cases, are responsible for cutting out the distribution channel. Reasons facilitating this increased co-operation include the dramatic improvement in the price and performance of database systems, better computer hardware, cheaper mass storage devices and improved data communications.

Approaches to supply chain management include:

- **Electronic Data Interchange (EDI)**: This is the interchange in electronic form of information, formerly provided on documents, between channel members. Benefits include reduced paperwork, improved accuracy, faster receipt of information, improved control of transportation and more stable relationships between trading partners. Many organisations now require that all their suppliers have an EDI capability. Most small Irish businesses will need to be EDI-compatible if they want to supply large multinationals and particularly the UK multiples.

- **Electronic Point of Sale (EPOS)**: This connects tills in retail outlets to a central computer that also handles warehouse control. This enables the distribution centre to go through the complete cycle of store replenishment with the correct calculated quantities after the last sale on one day and before the first sale of the next.

- **Electronic Funds Transfer at Point of Sale (EFTPOS)**: This enables customers to pay for their goods at the time of purchase, without cash and without writing a cheque that will take four days to process. Furthermore, accounting procedures, security and checkout efficiency are improved. These systems also provide considerable scope for marketing and merchandising strategies because of the information on individual customer shopping and purchasing habits that they can provide.

- **Radios, cellular phones, etc**: Communication within a warehouse by radio and by various forms of digital display. Communication with vehicles on the road by radio telephone and on-board fax machine.

- **Electronic Markets**: These use IT to disseminate information on prices, quantities and qualities of products, and buyers' and sellers' identities. Electronic markets may lower co-ordination costs for producers and retailers, lower physical distribution costs, or eliminate retailers and wholesalers entirely, as consumers directly access manufacturers.

MANAGING A SUCCESSFUL COLLABORATION

How should an entrepreneur manage a cooperative arrangement? The human element is the main reason for the success or failure of a cooperative arrangement. A good relationship has to be underpinned by the following:

- **Sharing of Information**: All partners must share information relevant to the partnership.

- **Relevance**: The issues that the alliance deal with must be important to both businesses.

- **Respect**: It is essential that all partners respect the ability and commitment of other partners.

- **Trust**: Trust is developed from a track record. In particular, it is important that partners maintain promises even when times are difficult.

- **Flexibility**: Partners must be willingness to listen. If necessary, they should be able to adapt and develop the relationship.

- **Understanding**: Each partner must have a clear understanding of where all the other partners stand.

CONCLUSION

Many entrepreneurs and small business have begun to respond to the changing commercial environment. This chapter outlined the various types of cooperative arrangements that might exist between businesses and the role of information technology in developing strategic alliances was reviewed. It should be noted that partnership strategies are a means to an end and not an end in themselves.

QUESTIONS

1. Discuss the different types of horizontal alliances.
2. When should entrepreneurs choose to collaborate rather than compete?

3. What do you understand by the term "Supply Chain Management"?

4. Discuss the importance of the role of information technology in alliances.

5. What factors are most influential to the success or failure of inter-firm collaboration?

REFERENCES

Chakravarthy, B. & P. Lorange (1991): *Managing the Strategy Process: A Framework for a Multibusiness Firm*, London: Prentice Hall.

10

Exploiting E-Commerce

Introduction

A revolution in communication technologies is sweeping the world — the next "industrial revolution". The revolution is centred around the technology that enables users to store, retrieve, process and communicate information, without having any due consideration about time and distance. This revolution will change the way people work, live and the way businesses compete. Entrepreneurs and small businesses can exploit these changes to improve their competitive position, enter new markets and reach new customers.

This chapter outlines how technological developments are affecting competition and our understanding of the marketplace. Market evolution is discussed and the shift from "marketplace" to "marketspace" explained. E-commerce is explained and strategies for small businesses to exploit the Internet are outlined.

The "Information Revolution"

The 12 million small and medium-sized enterprises in the EU need to manage information and management resources better. Easy-to-use and cost-effective networks that provide information and new market opportunities should improve the competitiveness of small businesses. Small businesses need to exploit new technologies to raise the efficiency of their management and production systems. These new electronic-based networks should assist small businesses in developing their commercial relationships with large companies. These networks should also help small businesses improve their R&D capabilities, through collaboration with universities and public and private research institutes. In addition, information networks should reduce the isolation of many of the SMEs in peripheral and less developed regions of the EU.

Figure 10.1: Expectations of the Information Age: An EU Perspective

---

- **Europe's Citizens and Consumers**: A caring society with a higher quality of life and a wider choice of services and entertainment.

- **Content Creators**: New ways for individuals to exercise their creativity as the information society results in new products and services.

- **Europe's Regions**: New opportunities to express cultural traditions and identities and, for those on the geographical peripheral of the Union, a minimising of distance and remoteness.

- **Government and Administration**: More efficient, transparent and responsive public service, which is closer to the citizen and which is provided at a lower cost.

- **European Business and SMEs**: More effective management and organisation, access to training and other services, including data links with customers and suppliers, which should result in improved competitiveness

- **European Telecommunications Operators**: The capacity to supply an ever-wider range of new high value added services.

- **Equipment and Software Suppliers**: New and growing markets for their products at home and abroad.

E-COMMERCE

This new emerging area has a plethora of definitions. E-commerce is described as the buying and selling of products, services and information via computer networks, including the internet (Turban, McClean and Weatherbe, 1999 and Laudon and Laudon, 1998). However, e-commerce has existed for over 25 years in the form of Electronic Data Interchange (EDI), facsimile and telephone transactions and video-text systems, like Mintel in France or BTX in Germany. The advent of the Internet is responsible for the increased activity in E-commerce. Some forecasts suggest that by 2003, e-commerce will account for 5% of retail sales worldwide, up from around 0.5% in 2000.

Figure 10.2: E-commerce Definitions

- Electronic commerce comprises functions of information exchange and commercial transaction support that operate on telecommunication networks linking business partners (typically, a customer and a supplier). It originated in the form of electronic data interchange (EDI) on value-added networks, based upon rigid and relatively complex specifications, and was generally imposed by large organisations upon their smaller suppliers. (Raymond and Bergeron,1996)

- E-commerce is the use of electronic transmission mediums (telecommunications) to engage in the exchange, including buying and selling, of products and services requiring transportation, either physically or digitally, from location to location. (Greenstein and Feinman, 2000)

- A modern business methodology that addresses the needs of organisations, merchants and consumers to cut costs while improving the quality of goods and services and increasing the speed of service delivery, by means of using information technology. (Kalakota and Whinston, 1997)

The definition of e-commerce can be further sub-divided into two main areas, business-to-business e-commerce (B2B) and business to consumer e-commerce (B2C). Business-to-business e-commerce refers to internet transactions between two or more businesses, including exchanges of information, products, services or payments (Solomon and Stuart, 2001). Business to consumer e-commerce refers to activities involving online transaction between companies and individual consumers. Examples of pure online B2C-based organisations are Amazon.com, Ebay.com, and Priceline.com.

Figure 10.3: Advantages and Challenges of E-Commerce for SMEs

---

Advantages

- Ability to compete with other companies locally, nationally and internationally.

- Creation of opportunities for more diverse people to start a business.

- Convenient and easy way of doing business transactions (24/7).

- A relatively inexpensive way for small business to compete.

Challenges

- Managing upgrades including business needs and applications.

- Adequate security for website and back end office functions.

- Avoiding being a victim of online fraud.

- Providing budget to maintain e-commerce presence.

- Retaining and training qualified staff.

Source: *E-Commerce Small Business Venture Online.* (1999) Washington, DC: US Small Business Administration Office of Advocacy.

SHIFTING MARKETS: FROM MARKETPLACE TO MARKETSPACE

Market Evolution

To understand the changes that are taking place as a result of the Information Age and e-commerce, it is necessary to understand the basic operations of the marketplace.

A market is the interaction between buyers and sellers. It is essentially a process of satisfying human needs, which involves producers and consumers. Consumers buy goods and services and, in some instances, they also work for the producers. The consumers and producers are in a twin demand and supply relationship with each other. The coming together of these two groupings is known as a market, be it a shop, a street market, an airline or a motor dealership (Figure 10.1). Most markets go through a number of common phases.

Figure 10.4: Market Transactions

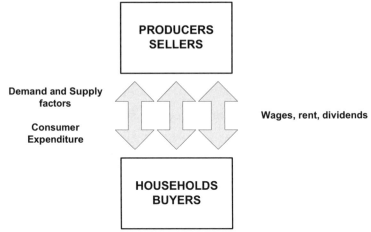

Market Emergence

A new market will usually emerge when there is a "disruption" point in an established market. At this stage, usually there is competition between the old and the new technologies. There may be a period of convergence with one technology dominating the market but, in some instances, some markets never achieve this. At this stage, there is a premium on flexibility. Businesses need to be responsive and to continuously innovate in order to exploit changes in the market. The actions of entrepreneurs and innovators often cause the emergence of new markets.

Market Growth

After the market emergence stage, new entrants are attracted by the prospect of high market growth. Innovations may be diffused within the market either quickly or slowly depending on:

- Barriers to adoption, for example patents, copyright, access to proprietary technology
- Actual and perceived risks of adopting the innovation
- Buyer access to relevant information
- Perceived advantage to be gained by entering the market.

The diffusion process can open up possibilities for further segmentation and reduce the uncertainty among potential buyers and entrants. Once the experience base accumulates, users of the product or service become well-informed about the product/service. In turn, this allows for further and broader diffusion to follow. Market forces tend to result in standardisation, due to product economies, which reduces the uncertainty and risk in the market. As its name suggests, this period of market growth is marked by high growth rates.

Slowing of Growth

The evolution of the market involves two reciprocal processes. Demand-side diffusion determines when and why buyers adopt the new products or services. Supply-side production impacts on the growth of the market and the entry and exit of competitors. The relationship between the supply-side and the demand-side in the market will dictate how fast or slowly the market grows. The over-riding factor in determining how fast a market grows is the density of competition competing for the same customer-base.

Market Consolidation

This phase in market evolution is likely to occur when the high growth rates become very visible and when there are few barriers to entry. The result of these factors is that the numbers of competitors will consolidate. Those competitors that are particularly vulnerable at this stage are sub-units of diversified companies and those companies who were pioneers or earlier specialists in the market. At this stage, competitors in the market are keenly focused on who will enter or exit the market. Potential entrants may be unknown and hence their intentions unclear.

Market Maturity

This is the last stage in the evolution of a market. At this stage, growth is very slow and there is increased concentration of the number of competitors. The market will be characterised by competitors with large economies of scale. In order to maintain their present market-share, competitors will concentrate on reducing their cost base through the application of technology. Increasingly-sophisticated marketing techniques will be used to identify customers. Existing or new competitors may identify untapped niche opportunities — for example, the development of convenience express stores on garage forecourts. Late arrivals may use a differentiated strategy— for example, Argos's entry into the Irish retail market.

Marketspace — the New Competitive Arena

The transactions and interactions between the buyers and sellers in the *marketplace* usually involve some physical interaction. However, the advent of the Information Age has meant that businesses need to rethink their concept of the marketplace. Many business transactions now occur outside traditional places of business. The whole notion of the *marketspace* is centred around information and electronic markets. Content, context and infrastructure are different in the marketspace:

- *Content* in the marketspace means that information about the product/service is available and not the actual product/service

- *Context* in the marketspace means that the transaction occurs using some form of electronic media

- *Infrastructure* enables the transactions to occur through the use of telecommunication and computer infrastructures.

In the marketspace, transactions between buyers and sellers are different because information is accessed and absorbed more easily by buyers, and because information and prices can be arranged in variety of formats. In the marketspace, businesses are not constrained by the traditional constraints of time, cost and location.

The benefits of the marketspace are outlined in Table 10.3.

The marketspace requires a new mind-set from those managing a business. It recasts how businesses create value for their customers. It also affects the linkages between a business and its external environment, in particular its customers. The marketspace is a radical shift in the method of transacting business for customers, since the interface has changed to an information-based format.

The key element for a small business attempting to develop its marketspace capability is getting its customers to transact their business through electronic formats. A small business can manage its interface with consumers by controlling the information content that customers or different stakeholders receive. Also, it maybe able to dictate the electronic format and type of infrastructure that is used to transact business.

However, it may be difficult to get customers to use the electronic marketspace because some customers may not have the computer and telecommunication facilities to interact in this marketspace. Also some customers will be unwilling to do business because it is impersonal.

Figure 10.5: The Benefits of the Marketspace

- **Lower Costs**: The provider of a product is not required to have the physical product on display.

- **Convenience**: The buyer can use electronic media to access information on various products/ services available from different sellers. This avoids time spent shopping around.

- **Ubiquity**: Products/services should become available everywhere because all potential buyers of the product/service can log-in into the electronic market.

- **Premium Prices**: The sellers of the product may be in a position to increase margins. Buyers may be willing to pay a premium over and above the prices charged in the physical marketplace. This is due to the fact that buyers have a greater selection to choose from and because they benefit from the convenience involved.

- **Manipulation of Brand Equity**: The content, context and infrastructure can all be manipulated simultaneously or separately in order to create value and brand loyalty.

- **Increased Sales**: The content of a website is accessible 24 hours a day seven days a week. It is estimated by the end of 2002 that e-commerce sales will have surpassed €300 Billion.

- **Level Playing Field**: All competitors in an industry have access to the Internet and can develop a e-commerce capability, regardless of their size.

- **Customer Loyalty**: Online buyers tend to return to the sites where they have bought before.

Small businesses cannot ignore this shift towards the marketspace. In many cases, small businesses first need to acknowledge that this shift is happening in their market and, second, need to develop a strategy to exploit these changes.

By using the marketspace, a business can bypass traditional third parties such as wholesalers and can interact directly with its customer-base. The business should benefit by receiving real time feedback and by increased control over the margins of its product/service.

*Figure 10.6: E-Commerce Adoption Among Irish SMEs —
Golden and Griffin*

The main findings of the Golden and Griffin research were:

- 46% of SMEs believe that their Internet site is providing value for money, while 24% believe it is not.

- 12% of firms are generating over 1,000 hits per week to their website, while 34% are receiving less than 50 hits per week. Firms with higher number of hits are generating higher turnovers from their websites.

- 13% of firms are generating over €317 a month directly from their internet site. 28% of firms are generating no sales revenue from their website and a further 47% don't know what turnover their Internet site is adding to the business.

- 26% spent more than €2,539 on the initial design of their web pages while 22% of firms spent less than €317. Those organisations that spent more initially on the design of their web pages have a larger number of hits to their site. However, increased spending and the resultant number of hits does not result in a higher turnover directly attributable to the website.

- 28% regard the provision of electronic commerce support by ISPs as important. This shows that the majority of SMEs are not interested in selling directly on-line. Rather, the key reason for developing a website is to advertise the firm to a wider set of potential customers.

GOING ONLINE

The Internet can be a powerful tool for a business and has created a unique marketing channel. A combination of the falling costs of computers and cheaper access costs has meant that most businesses have the ability to access and run websites. Small businesses have been fast to adapt, recognising that there are many benefits of using the Internet (Figure 10.8).

However, many have set up Internet sites without proper consideration of the impact this may have on the business and its customers. Using the Internet is not passive like TV, as it requires the participation of the user. The key for a business considering using the Internet is to establish what motivates the users to access particular sites? For a website to be successful, particularly as a marketing site, there must be a reason for the user to visit it. The objective is to keep users interested in the site and to stimulate repeat visits.

Figure 10.7: Blarney Woollen Mills goes Online

Blarney Woollen Mills (BWM) specialises in Irish garments, gifts and crafts. The company has retail outlets in Cobh, Dublin, Killarney and Kilkenny and trades under the names of The Kilkenny Shop, Club Tricot and The Sweater Shop. Their flagship complex, which includes a retail shop, a hotel and a restaurant, is located in Blarney, County Cork. The business has a mail order business based in Blarney as well as having a New Jersey-based distribution centre for US mail order business. BWM has attempted to target its products at the tourist market. It has established its marketing presence at points of entry to Ireland, through sponsored maps (national and city maps) and se-lected advertising. The mail order division targets potential buyers in the US through catalogues.

BWM's first exposure to Internet technologies was a visit by senior management to Kenny's Book Shop in Galway. This small shop had begun to sell Irish books on the Internet. BWM decided to establish an Internet presence. After a formal business analysis BWM selected Ieu-net as their service provider and began to create a web site. The IT de-partment of the company was involved initially to assist in technical matters. The overall strategy that guided this Web presence design was shopping, culture and tourism designed to complement their overall marketing strategy. The site consisted of a home page with graphic images of the Mill Complex in Blarney and hypertext links to Tourism, Culture, On-line Catalogue and History pages. One of the primary aims of the web site for BWM was to get people to visit the page and have a reason to return. Another element was to integrate Internet marketing with the company's other marketing elements. The tourism page is designed to provide tourist information similar to BWM's printed maps and guides. Links to holiday destinations where BWM's has shops and information on entertainment, activities and sports are also provided. The cultural page initially had information on Ireland and the history pages outlines the development of the or-ganisation from its beginnings.

The on-line shopping catalogue, Virtual Shopping Guide to Ire-land, includes information on crafts, gift-ware, men's and women's fashion items. This page allows the consumer to order the products on-line, and allows the consumer to choose between use of major credit cards or alternatively contact BMW directly by phone.

BWM's presence on the WWW raised the group's profile on a world-wide basis, as they often received e-mail requests asking for catalogues. In addition, many of their international visitors to their retail outlets in Ireland frequently mentioned that they have seen the BWM site on the Internet. Furthermore, the early experiments with an Internet strategy meant that there was a surge in the internal mail system, as nearly all of the BWM's group entities now use e-mail for inter-group communication. BWM consider the overall cost of establishing a web presence as nominal. The largest element was the design consultant's fee and the addition of a modem. Internet costs for connection are considered minimal but there is the additional cost of employing personnel to update the pages and respond to e-mail requests.

Figure 10.8: Benefits of the Internet

- Eliminates time and geographical barriers.
- Provides the firm with a cheap form of communications.
- Documents can be sent anywhere within in minutes via FTP.
- Enables closer interaction with the different stakeholders in the business.
- A better international profile even though the venture maybe operating from a small base.
- Customers can order products and service through a new mechanism.
- Some savings can be made as it reduces the amount of paper and colour finished brochures about the firm's products and services.
- Some customers may perceive that potential clients may view them as at the leading edge of technology.

Not all products/services are suitable for the Internet. For a small business to assess the suitability of the Internet for its markets it needs to consider:

- **Cultural Differences**: The audience the business is trying to target may be spread over a number of countries. From a cultural perspective, they may be unwilling or slower to use the Internet as a medium to transact business. The US culture means people are accustomed to buying goods from mail order companies over the telephone and the Internet is merely another platform where transactions can occur.

- **Linguistic Capabilities**: The different linguistic backgrounds of the business's audience may require the development of the same site in a number of different languages.

- **Access to Technology**: Does the audience the business is attempting to attract have access to the Internet? The business must consider the cost of access from the user's perspective. The state of the telecommunications network locally may mean that some potential customers cannot access the Internet or that the access cost via the telecommunications infrastructure may be prohibitive for home use.

- **Demographics**. Is the product aimed at people who have grown up without any exposure to computers and the Internet?

Figure 10.9: Findings from ICT Gaeltacht Survey

- 60% of respondents used the Internet either at home or at work/in an educational setting (or both).

- One in three respondents used the Internet in the home and at work, while only one in 10 accessed the medium solely at home.

- 30% of respondents used the Internet several times a day.

- 30% of respondents used the Internet several times a week.

- 38% of respondents used the Internet for emailing, which was the highest use of the Internet.

- 38% did not have the Internet at home or do not use it more often due to the ongoing cost of access.

Source: Information and Communications Technologies in the Gaeltacht, (2000): Mílaois Na Gaeltacht and Údarás Na Gaeltachta — research carried out by NUI, Galway.

Getting on the Internet

How can a small business develop its presence on the Internet? Many businesses develop their own Internet sites. Technological developments have resulted in a rise in the entry-level standards for businesses developing a presence on the Internet.

The stages of developing an Internet presence are:

Phase 1: Identify the Opportunity

The small business has to decide whether it needs a presence on the Internet. This decision should be in line with the overall strategic direction of the business. So why should a small business consider linking up to the Internet? (Table 10.5)

Ryanair saw the opportunity of using the Internet as a source of revenue, a means to cut out the travel agents and a medium to assist the company in lowering its cost-base (www.ryanair.com). As part of the restructuring of Aer Lingus, senior management have considered adopting the Ryanair e-commerce model of interacting with its customers for booking of airline seats on its flights (www.aerlingus.com). Moreover, a number of small real estate agents identified the opportunities and benefits the Internet brought to their business and developed, with AIB, the property website, my.home.ie.

Figure 10.10: Reasons to use the Internet

- *Information* about competitors is readily available.
- Portrays a *professional image* to prospective customers.
- Can be used as a *marketing tool* for a small business that operates in specialised global markets.
- *Easy to communicate* with other organisations, and various stakeholders of the business.
- Provides a *medium to provide information* on the business and its product/service.
- *Other organisations can access information* regarding the business.
- Provides a means of *distributing products/services.*
- Provides a platform to *obtain business intelligence* about suppliers.
- It may *generate extra revenue* for the business and/or increase margins.
- The *cost base of the firm may be reduced.*
- Enables the business to receive *timely feedback* from potential customers or clients.

Phase 2: Developing the Strategy

During this stage, the business starts to develop the material required for the Internet. The business needs to be sure that it has the technical capabilities to do this. Typically, the drive to develop an Internet presence comes from marketing personnel or from staff with computer expertise. The content of the pages is usually a split between marketing and information-based elements, containing information about the history of the business, its products/services, press releases, financial highlights, locations and contact names within the business.

However, some companies go beyond essential information content and give the customer an opportunity to buy the product or service. For example, Hughes' Supermarket in Claregalway, County Galway, has a website that allow customers to buy groceries online.

Figure 10.11: Assessing the Venture's Competencies and Benefits of the Internet

- What are the benefits of the Internet access?
- Does the target market have access to this form of technology?
- How is the firm going ensure that their web site is accessible to the target market via the various search engines?
- What are the costs of the Internet access and the development of the web pages?
- What are the risks to the businesses in terms of security (viruses, unauthorised access) and business risks such as lack of sponsorship, poor quality site, underdeveloped back up services and lack of channel support?

Phase 3: Developing and Testing the Prototype

Once the business has established a basic, good quality website, it should seek feedback from external and internal users.

Before launching the site, the small business may ask a number of users to test the service over a period of time and to provide feedback of various elements of the site, such as page layout, links within the site, the use of graphics, payment systems and the overall security of the website.

Usually, somebody will be given the responsibility to collect data for the site, to update it on a regular basis and to experiment by adding additional services such as on-line marketing and selling of products/services.

Figure 10.12: 12Travel.com – Explore, Dream and Discover[12]

12Travel.com is an online travel agency based in West Cork, providing inbound holidays and package tours. The company was founded in 1998 when Conor B. Buckley, Conor Buckley and Cormac O'Neill decided to return to Ireland after four years of working and studying in the United States. Although they lived in Philadelphia, they booked their round-the-world trip from a travel agent in San Francisco, whom they had located on the Internet. They realised that there was an opening and opportunity for travel services over the Internet. Conor B. Buckley was give a premises by his parents at his home outside Skibbereen, from which he conducted the day-to-day running of the company.

During 1999, the company obtained its travel agency licence, and went live with its website employing four experienced travel consultants. 12Travel.com made its first sale to an American couple going on honeymoon. Staff grew to 28 employees, consisting of web designers, travel consultants, product developers, a technical writer and a public relations officer. Moreover, the company developed websites for the British, German and Canadian markets, which were launched in 2000. 12Travel.com enjoyed 500% growth between June 1999 and June 2000. Furthermore, they strengthened the management structure of the company with appointments of Dan Byrne (he spent much of his career at Apple and rose to be managing director of Apple Europe) as chairman of the board and Alf Smiddy (currently managing director of Beamish & Crawford) and Mr. Roddy Feely (he played a key role in the Irish Tourist Board through his 40-year tenure) as non executive directors. In its first full year of trading, it achieved over €1.26 million in sales. The company also won the won the West Cork Enterprise Award and a Golden Spider Award, which is given to websites showing excellence in their design and functionality.

---

[12] The authors wish to acknowledge the contribution of Niamh Sheedy, a Diploma in Business Studies student at National University of Ireland, Galway (2000).

Phase 4: Delivering and Maintaining the Service

In this phase, the business enters the reality of e-commerce. This phase requires a radical shift in thinking, as the principals of the business will have to consider the electronic format as a new arena of competition. The key elements of this phase in Internet development are outlined in Table 10.7.

Figure 10.13: Key Elements in Delivering and Maintaining the Service

- Internal systems within the business must be responsive to the electronic channels as well as the current channels of supply and delivery.
- Employees of the business must be made aware of their roles and responsibilities with this new channel.
- The business should be examining the possibility of developing their existing links to other stakeholders thereby locking them into the organisation.
- The business should develop plans to further develop existing electronic channels.

THE CHALLENGE OF THE DIGITAL DIVIDE

The Internet will soon be so pervasive that not having access to the technology or not knowing how to use it will be the equivalent of not knowing how to read or write The digital divide for e-commerce is not homogenous but reflects a combination of wider historical social inequities and emerging telecommunications network access issues. Tackling the digital divide requires a proactive policy environment that recognises the source of exclusion and the inhibiting factors. In this regard, research carried out on behalf of Mílaois Na Gaeltacht and Údarás Na Gaeltachta identified six main digital divides.

Technology Divide

There are three divides regarding access to technology and infrastructure.

The first is simple access. This is where citizens have access to basic telecommunications infrastructure through, for example, a digital telephone exchange. The next divide that separates citizens is experience. This is where more experienced citizens tap the benefits of the internet fully. The last divide centres on those citizens who have high speed access to telecommunications infrastructure, through cable and other broadband delivery systems.

Underpinning the technology divide are the cost of access, the speed and reliability of the communications services and the availability of ICT.

Rural/Urban Divide

ICT tracking measurements from other countries indicate a divide between Internet usage in rural areas as opposed to urban areas. Rural households tend to have a lower penetration rate in accessing the Internet than urban areas due, in the main, to the telecommunications infrastructure deficit.

Household Income Divide

All income levels have some access to the Internet, be it in a work or home environment. However, the rates of home connections to the Internet are higher at middle-income levels than any other level. In addition, these middle-income households have the highest growth rate in terms of Internet connection and usage.

Furthermore, a large gap remains regarding Internet penetration rates among householders of different races and ethic origins.

Education Divide

The availability of ICT across every education level has accelerated its usage. Households headed by someone with education experience showed the greatest expansion in Internet penetration.

However, early school leavers, women working in the home, the elderly and the unemployed are still marginalized regarding ICT.

Gender Divide

Until recently, there was a disparity in Internet usage between men and women. Men were greater users of the technology than women. However, by August 2000, 44.6% of men and a statistically indistinguishable 44.2% of women were Internet users in the US.

Age Divide

Citizens over 50 years of age are less likely to use the Internet than other age groups, while younger citizens experience one of the highest growth rates in Internet usage. Even among younger citizens, there is a gap between different races and ethic origins.

CONCLUSION

There have been rapid changes in technology and increasing global-isation of markets. These changes create risks and opportunities for SME businesses. In particular, new information technologies provide small businesses with a low cost way of selling to and supporting cus-tomers globally. In this shift from marketplace to marketspace, there is one constant — that markets continue to become more competitive.

QUESTIONS

1. How can small businesses best exploit the Information Revolution?
2. What do you understand by the terms "e-commerce", "marketplace" and "marketspace"?
3. What benefits might a small business get from going on-line?
4. Prepare a strategy for an SME planning to use the Internet?
5. Identify a web site by "surfing the net" and outline the strengths and weaknesses of this site.

REFERENCES

Solomon. M and Stuart, E. (2001). The Brave New World of E-Commerce for Marketing: Real People Real Choices, Prentice Hall: Saddle River, NJ.

Turban, E., McLean, E. and Weatherbe, J. (1999). *Information Technology for Management: Making Connections for Strategic Advantage*, John Wiley: New York.

Laudon, K and Laudon, J. (1998). *Management Information Systems*, Prentice Hall: Saddle River, NJ.

Raymond, L. and Bergeron, F., (1996). "EDI success in small and medium-sized enterprises: a field study", *Journal of Organizational Computing and Electronic Commerce*, 6 : 2.

Greenstein, M. and Feinman, T.M. (2000). *Electronic Commerce: Security, Risk Management and Control*, McGraw-Hill: New York

Kalakota, R. and Whinston, A.B. (1997). *Electronic Commerce: A Manager's Guide*, Addison-Wesley: Boston, MA.

Golden G., and Griffin M. (1998) *A Survey of Internet Commerce in Small and Medium Sized Enterprises*, National University of Ireland, Galway.

Information and Communication Technologies in the Gaeltacht Areas 2001-2006 (2000); Mílaois Na Gaeltacht and Údarás Na Gaeltachta.

11

ENCOURAGING AND SUPPORTING ENTREPRENEURSHIP

INTRODUCTION

There is a widely held believe that Irish society is anti-enterprise and that it is difficult to be a successful entrepreneur in Ireland. The social standing of entrepreneurs in Ireland has traditionally been low and they are often referred as "gangsters and chancers". In contrast to these beliefs, the evidence suggests that Ireland is a nation of small businesses. Of the 190,000 businesses in Ireland 98% employ less than 50 and have a turnover of less than €4.5 million. Over 90% of all businesses employ less than ten staff.

This chapter explores the factors that determine the level of entrepreneurship in a society or a region. Each of these factors is discussed in detail. This is followed by a review of the State agencies that support new and small businesses. The findings of the Task Force on Small Business and of the Culliton Report are presented, which provide the backdrop to the development of entrepreneurship in Irish society.

FACTORS THAT INFLUENCE ENTREPRENEURSHIP

During the last four decades, countries have produced very different rates of economic growth and prosperity. The extent and type of entrepreneurial activity in an economy is an important determinant of overall national wealth. How can entrepreneurial activity be encouraged? There are a number of factors that determine the level of entrepreneurial activity in an economy (Figure 11.1). There are two basic explanations for the level of enterprise in an economic region:

- The first explanation is that economic conditions determine the level of enterprise. A lack of economically viable opportunities discourages people from starting businesses. The implicit assumption of this explanation is that, as opportunities appear, people will act to exploit them. This is referred to as the "demand" side argument. Many of Margaret Thatcher's economic and social policies were based on this argument. Her belief was that people would start businesses and work harder if the right economic incentives existed.

- The contrasting explanation is that the "supply" of entrepreneurs is determined by cultural and social factors. The assumption underlying this explanation is that entrepreneurs have certain psychological characteristics, which are developed in individuals by the social and cultural conditions that they live in. These characteristics take time to develop and therefore the "supply" of entrepreneurs is considered to be "fixed" in the short run.

Figure 11.1: The Determinants of Entrepreneurship

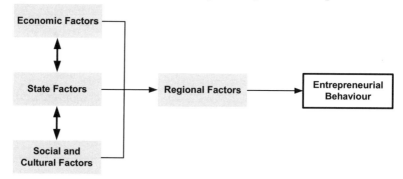

Figure 11.2: Start-up rate of enterprises in the EU and US for 1986–1990 (expressed as a percentage of existing enterprises).

	1986	1987	1988	1989	1990
Belgium	7.0	9.3	12.3	12.3	10.9
Denmark	15.8	13.8	14.3	14.4	14.3
Germany	16.4	16.7	17.7	18.3	20.1
Italy	8.7	8.1	7.2	6.6	6.5
Luxembourg	14.4	13.3	13.3	14.4	—
Netherlands	11.7	12.7	13.5	14.4	14.5
Portugal	9.5	11.0	12.3	10.7	—
UK	13.3	14.2	15.7	16.2	14.2
US	14.2	14.4	13.6	13.5	13.8
IRELAND	**13.6**	**11.6**	**12.9**	**13.9**	**12.9**

Figure 11.3: Are the Irish Entrepreneurial?

> *It is very difficult to measure the level of enterprise in a society. Anecdotal evidence would suggest that some societies, for example the US, are much more entrepreneurial than Irish society. Research evidence is inconclusive as it is impossible to count the number of new business start-ups. Research is usually based on the number of new company registrations. However, this is inaccurate as many businesses have a number of different legal companies for tax and administrative reasons. Additionally, not all new start-ups register as companies.*
>
> *The Task Force on Small Business suggests that the rate of start-up of new businesses in Ireland is similar to the US, the UK, and to Continental European countries. This evidence is based on the number of VAT registrations. The Task Force evidence on the rate of closure suggests that, within five tears of establishment, 40 percent of businesses will have ceased to trade. Furthermore, within nine years of establishment, 56 percent of all businesses will have ceased trading. The rate of failure is highest during years two and three.*
>
> *However, these aggregate figures conceal the type of businesses that are being created. There is an argument that, in Ireland, there is a shortage of start-ups in innovative and high technology sectors and that not enough start-ups have high growth potential.*

Economic Factors Influencing Entrepreneurship

Entrepreneurial behaviour is influenced by the number and type of market opportunities, if there are few business opportunities, there will be little enterprise. However, even if there are lots of opportunities, entrepreneurs will only exploit them if they are perceived to be profitable. The profit potential of an opportunity is dependent on both the cost of supplying the market, the size and nature of the market.

The Profit Potential of an Entrepreneurial Opportunity: Costs

The significant costs in a new business are the cost of capital and of labour. Other important costs are raw materials, transport, telecommunications and land. An entrepreneur will implicitly calculate the cost of these factors before starting a business. The cost of these factors is determined by their availability and, in some cases, by Government actions. The cost of doing business is higher in most European countries than it is in the US. For example, in Europe, the cost of labour is high due to Government regulations and taxes; the cost of capital has traditionally been high due to poor budgetary management; and the costs of telecommunications and transport have been high due to regulation and inefficient State-owned monopolies.

In considering a specific market opportunity, an entrepreneur will need to consider the barriers to entry. Barriers to entry include large capital requirements, product differentiation, and access to distribution channels. These barriers can make it more difficult and expensive to enter a market. Often entrepreneurs don't identify the barriers to entry. For example, in the food sector, many "product driven" entrepreneurs fail because they don't identify access to distribution channels and the capital needed to build a brand as barriers to entry.

The Profit Potential of an Entrepreneurial Opportunity: Revenues

The size and nature of market demand influences the decision to start a business. Economies that are characterised by many market opportunities will encourage entrepreneurs to start-up new businesses. Deregulation can create new market opportunities. Companies such as Ryanair, Esat Digifone (now O2) and FM104 have been created to respond to industry deregulation. The State can increase or decrease the number of opportunities by changing the level of regulation that is required to start-up and operate a business.

Social & Cultural Factors Influencing Entrepreneurship [13]

The level and type of entrepreneurial activity in an economy is influenced by social and cultural factors. These factors may foster and encourage the traits necessary for entrepreneurship. Such traits include initiative, energy, independence, boldness, self-reliance and willingness to take risks. If enterprise is encouraged as an overall approach to life, it will become a part of the norms and values held by the society. An enterprise culture is one in which the acquisition of these qualities is both highly valued and extensively practiced. The following are social and cultural factors that influence entrepreneurial behaviour:

- **Legitimacy of Entrepreneurship**: Legitimacy refers to the degree to which certain modes of behaviour are accepted by a society. A society with a high degree of legitimacy of entrepreneurship encourages people to learn about enterprise and to exploit this knowledge by engaging in entrepreneurship. The

---

[13] The authors acknowledge the contribution of Joseph Gannon, Business Research Programme, The Michael Smurfit Graduate School of Business, University College Dublin, to this section.

level of legitimacy of entrepreneurship varies between societies. The US is a society that actively encourages entrepreneurial activity. The degree of legitimacy accorded to entrepreneurship determines who engages in it. Where there is high legitimacy, entrepreneurship will be dominated by the people from "mainstream" society. The lower the legitimacy, the more likely it is that entrepreneurs will come from socially-marginal groups.

- **Social Marginality**: In many societies, it is those in marginal groups that act most entrepreneurially. Many marginal groups are more entrepreneurial because they are restricted from traditional career paths and social routes. Marginality maybe in terms of religion or ethnic background. However, not all marginal groups act entrepreneurially. For members of a marginal group to choose entrepreneurship as a career, it is necessary that there is a high level of legitimacy for entrepreneurship within the group.

- **Social Mobility**: Social mobility is the degree of mobility within the social structure. Social mobility is high if people within a society can change social roles and occupations. Mobility is low if people find it difficult to change careers and change social status. Blocks to mobility may be social or geographical. There are several different views as to how social mobility impacts on the emergence of entrepreneurship. Firstly, there is an argument that high mobility encourages entrepreneurship. As it gets easier to move up and down the social structure, more people will choose entrepreneurship as a career path. The "American Dream" is an articulation of an aspiration for a society with high social mobility. Secondly, there is an argument that low mobility encourages individuals to act entrepreneurially. People choose entrepreneurship because traditional career paths are blocked to them. This is often referred to as "social blockage". Overall, it may be the case that it is necessary to have some combination of both flexibility and rigidity in social mobility.

State Factors Influencing Entrepreneurship
Government influences the level of entrepreneurship in a number of ways by:

- Determining the nature of market conditions and the cost of exploiting market opportunities
- Influencing social and cultural factors

- Acting entrepreneurially itself. The nature of the system of governance also has an effect on the level of entrepreneurial activity.

The most important factor is the relationship between central and local government, in particular the autonomy of local government. Ireland is one of the most centralised democracies in Western Europe. Central Government dominates and there is virtually no autonomy at local level. Greater local autonomy should result in regions and individuals taking responsibility for their own economic welfare.

State's Impact on Economic Factors

The State influences the attractiveness of business opportunities in a number of ways:

- **As a Purchaser of Capital**: The State increases the cost of capital to competing users such as entrepreneurs and industry by purchasing capital. The State needs to purchase capital to fund State expenditure and to pay-off national debts. In Ireland, the State raises capital in many ways, for example through the sale of Government Bonds, An Post saving schemes.

- **By Setting Interest Rates**: The Government may use interest rates as a means of controlling inflation. Lower interest rates mean that it is cheaper to raise capital and to start a business. The single-figure interest rates of recent years have made many business opportunities more attractive. In Ireland, following monetary union, the Government has a decreasing influence on interest rate policy, since interest rates are now determined by the European Central Bank.

- **The Tax System**: The tax system has a significant impact on the ability of people to save and accumulate resources. These savings may become the seed capital for a future business. Also the tax system can determine the potential return people will earn, which in turn affects investment decisions. In Ireland, Government policy initiatives such as offering tax breaks for owners of city centre car parks and apartments resulted in an increase in economic activity in these sectors.

- **Competition Policy**: The enforcement of a tough competition policy in the marketplace by the Government can ensure that there are more opportunities for business. Recent deregulation in many industries has created new business opportunities.

- **As a Purchaser of Goods and Services**: The Government, as a significant purchaser of goods, can create significant opportunities for small businesses. This requires the buyers in Government departments to consider purchasing from smaller companies. Under EU law, the Government cannot discriminate in favour of Irish businesses when purchasing goods and services.

- **Grants and Financial Assistance**: The State has a direct impact on the cost and availability for capital for many entrepreneurs through the provision of grants and "soft loans". A grant is a form of free capital. The objective of these incentives is to make it more attractive and profitable to start a business. Financial assistance may be in the form of grants, subsidised loans, equity investments, and tax relief. This financial assistance may be given for a specific purpose, such as research & development, marketing, or feasibility studies. In many cases, the rules and regulations governing State assistance makes it unattractive to potential entrepreneurs.

- **Laws and Regulations**: The Government has control over many of the laws and regulations that impact on business. Amendments to these could make it simpler to do business in Ireland, for example the tax system could be simplified.

- **"Prompt Payment" Legislation**: Slow payment by debtors increases the working capital requirement of small businesses. In Ireland, the State is now attempting to reduce the dependency of many small businesses on bank borrowings by enacting "Prompt Payment" legislation. This requires businesses to pay their creditors on time. Failure to do so means the invoice attracts an immediate interest charge. Prompt Payment legislation exists in many other countries.

State's Impact on Social & Cultural Factors

The role of the Government in encouraging enterprise is crucial. Government ideology has a significant impact on the choices the Government will make in terms of taxation and spending policies. The most visible difference between political parties is in their attitude towards the role of the State and the extent to which it intervenes in public life. The attitudes of Government towards entrepreneurial activity can increase the overall legitimacy of entrepreneurship.

The Government controls the education system. This is often an under-utilised policy instrument. The education system has a significant impact on people's career choices. In Ireland, the education system could be more proactive in suggesting self-employment as a legitimate career option, although, in recent years, the Irish Government has begun to introduce enterprise into the secondary school curriculum.

State's Impact as an Entrepreneur

Historically, the State in Ireland has acted entrepreneurially by creating many State and semi-State companies, for example companies such as Bord na Mona, Irish Sugar (now Greencore), Irish Shipping (now Irish Ferries), ACC Bank (now part of Rabobank), and ICC Bank (now part of Bank of Scotland), Telecom Eireann (now eircom) were all created by the State. It is a Government policy that the semi-States should develop their commercial mandate. Currently, the Government is looking to privatise many of the remaining semi-State companies.

Regional Factors

Role Models

Role models influence entrepreneurs both directly and indirectly. A successful entrepreneurial role model in a region or locality may encourage and justify entrepreneurial activity in general. Role models can also directly impact on the level of entrepreneurship by providing encouragement, advice and finance to perspective entrepreneurs. There are some well-known role models in Ireland, for example Noel C. Duggan, Fergal Quinn of Superquinn, and Gillian Bowler, the founder of Budget Travel. Unfortunately, in many rural areas in Ireland, the successful role model is often the person who emigrated and succeeded in the US or the UK.

Local Infrastructure & Support Services

The presence of a basic local infrastructure is essential if entrepreneurial activity is to occur. Research in the UK has suggested that an increase in the availability of low-cost, small premises results in increased entrepreneurial activity. In many regions in Ireland, including some cities, it can be difficult to get low-cost premises when starting up. The lack of availability of skilled and trained staff may also prevent the development of a business.

The Government may provide business advice directly, through a mentoring scheme or by grant-aiding the purchase of such advice and expertise. The main areas in which start-ups and small businesses require assistance are marketing, financial management and strategic management. A mentoring scheme encourages experienced businesspeople to support entrepreneurs and small businesspeople by offering advice.

Incubator Organisations

Entrepreneurs will normally have gained a significant amount of work experience before they start their new businesses. The presence of suitable businesses in a locality will impact on the business experiences of entrepreneurs. The type of business that this experience is gained in is important. There are a number of factors that influence whether an employee will leave a business and start-up on their own:

- *Size of the Business*: Research evidence has shown that entrepreneurs tend to have work experience in small rather than large businesses. The reason for this maybe that managers in small businesses are exposed to more functional areas. There is much more specialisation in large companies and it is common for staff to work in only one functional area.

- *Business Sector*: Some sectors have a higher "spin-off" rate than others. Sectors with high barriers to entry have lower spin-off rates, for example the drinks sector. Sectors with lower barriers to entry, for example the software sector, tend to have a high "spin-off" rate.

STATE SUPPORT OF ENTERPRISE

Government Policy on Enterprise

A number of reports have influenced the Government's thinking and policies on entrepreneurship. Although almost a decade old, the two reports reviewed below were largely responsible for the current enterprise landscape.

The Culliton Report

The Industrial Policy Review Group, chaired by Jim Culliton, issued its report in 1992. In this, Culliton argued that it is "time to accept that the solutions to our problems lie in our hands. We need to foster a spirit of self-reliance and determination to take charge of our future".

Recommendations from the Culliton Report included:

- **Taxation**: The Report recommended that the tax system should be reviewed fundamentally on a phased but continual basis. It recommended that the tax base be broadened by abolishing many tax reliefs, exemptions and deductions. Specifically, the group recommended that the standard tax rate be extended, resulting in fewer people paying tax at the higher rate. It suggested the taxation system be reformed to ensure that there were fewer distortions between the numerous savings options.

- **Infrastructure**: The Report argued that, without the proper infrastructure, it would be difficult for business to operate. The three most important aspects of infrastructure are transport, communications and energy costs. The Report argued that it is important that State-protected monopolies be induced to operate efficiently, as the cost of their inefficiency is passed on to industry. Furthermore, it suggested that there is a need for Irish ports to be made more competitive and for energy costs to be minimised. Specifically, the Report recommended that the Irish Government be more proactive in developing Ireland's environmental policies and should build on its green image, rather than reacting to developments.

- **Education, Enterprise and Technology**: The Report recognised that education and training are a critical element of Government policy that affect not only industry but our overall economic welfare. The Report argued that the education system has become increasingly academic in nature and that the system needs to de-emphasis this bias towards the liberal arts and the traditional professions. It suggested that, within the education system, a high priority should be attached to the transfer of usable and marketable skills. The Report recommended that a high quality and respected stream of technical and vocational education be developed. This stream would operate with close ties to industry. The Report recommended that grants be given for general training schemes for the existing workforce. It suggested that the State training agency, FÁS, needed to separate its "training for industry" function from its "support for the unemployed" function.

- **Direct Support for Industry**: The Report recognised that the activities of the numerous State agencies involved in supporting industry are now less important then they used to be. Specifically, the Report recommended that the budgets for grants for attracting overseas companies should be reduced. Grants for indigenous industry should be replaced with equity investments by the State where possible. The Report suggested that grants should be focused on supporting clusters of related industries. The report concluded that the commercial State enterprises need access to more capital for investment.

- **Institutional Strengthening**: The Report recommended that the Department of Industry and Commerce (now Enterprise, Trade and Employment) should redefine its role. Its new role should be to develop and implementing policy for industrial development and the creation of a business-related legal and regulatory environment. In redefining its role, the Department would need to reduce some of its existing activities and to place greater emphasis on employing people with industrial experience. The Report recommended that, within the Industrial Development Authority, the role of supporting indigenous industry and that of attracting overseas investment should be separated (this lead to the creation of Enterprise Ireland to support indigenous industry, and IDA Ireland to attract inwards investment).

- **Food Industry**: The Report specifically examined the food industry because of its importance to the Irish economy. The Report recommended that the food sector needs to achieve the lowest cost of production possible that is consistent with a high quality; that the problem of seasonal milk production needs to be addressed; and that the "green" image of Irish food needs to be developed.

Many of these recommendations have now been implemented.

The Task Force on Small Business
The Task Force on Small Business issued its report in 1994. Its key recommendations included:

- **Raising Money**: The Task Force recognised that sourcing funds can be difficult for many small businesses. Many small business people argue that there is a shortage of funds available. Many small businesses are not financially attractive to lending institutions because of the high level of risk and high relative administrative costs for the bank. The sources of finance used by most new and small business are personal savings. When most small businesses try to expand, they rely on internally-generated profits. However, the tax system constrains the ability of individuals to save and to therefore to reinvest in their business. The Irish taxation system encourages people to choose high-return low-risk projects. As a result, a small business-owner might achieve a higher capital gain on their personal home than on the

increase in the value of their business. The Task Force's
recommendations were:

◊ The establishment of a loan fund that would lend specifically to
   small business. A number of these loan funds have been
   created, for example the ICC €126 million Small Business
   Expansion Loan Scheme. These funds provide long-term loans
   to small business.

◊ Tax relief should be given for investments made prior to start-
   up. This recommendation was included by the Government in
   the 1997 budget. Entrepreneurs can now claim expenses made
   prior to start-up as taxable expenses.

◊ Money from the County Enterprise Boards should only given
   with the appointment of a mentor to the business.

- **Prompt Payment**: The ability to get paid affects the capital
  requirements of a small business. The Task Force showed that the
  average number of days required for payment in Ireland is 79
  days, nearly two-and-a-half months. Since this is only an average,
  there are many customers who are even slower than this. The
  Task Force recommended that "Prompt Payment" legislation be
  enacted for the public sector in Ireland. Seven of the EU member
  States have mandatory rules governing payment times and terms
  for Government purchases. The Task Force believed similar
  legislation for the private sector would be too difficult to enforce.

- **Rewarding Risk**: The Task Force recommended that the
  Government address the relationship between risk and return for
  small business-owners. The level of failure in new and small
  business is high. Within five years of start-up, over 50 percent of
  companies will have failed. In addition to investing their own
  capital, most small business owners work more than 55 hours a
  week. The financial return they receive for this work, for investing
  their capital, and for taking a risk, is low. The Task Force
  recommended that the tax on profits be reduced, that the rate of
  capital gains tax on the disposal of a business should be reduced,
  and that small businesses should receive tax breaks for increasing
  employment.

- **Reducing Burdens**: The Task Force recommended that the State
  reduce the regulatory burdens on small business. It costs a small
  business more than a large business to comply with the regulatory
  requirements of the State. The time the entrepreneur spends
  complying with the paperwork required by the State could be

better spent trying to develop the business. Many small business owners are reluctant or are unable to delegate this activity. The Task Force suggested that small firms find it difficult to comply with many labour regulations, many of which are designed from a large company perspective. The Task Force recommended that the burdens on small business be reduced in a number of ways:

◊   A reduction in number of forms to be completed by consolidating existing forms

◊   The simplification of forms

◊   The removal of the requirement for small firms to produce audited accounts

◊   A simplified Company Registration & Incorporation procedure for new small companies.

• **Providing Help**: The Task Force recommended that there should be a single point of contact for all advice and assistance for small businesses. This contact point should also provide basic information about what is required to start-up and manage a small business. The Task Force recommended that greater attention should be provided to developing the management skills of owner-mangers, since this is the biggest problem facing most small businesses. To date, the help received by small businesses has focused on providing finance. The Task Force showed that Irish companies lost market-share to importers during the previous decade. The Task Force identified a number of market opportunities for small businesses: government departments and agencies; sub-supply linkages with larger companies; and sales direct to end-users.

• **A New Deal for Small Business**: The Task Force recommended that there should be greater attention focused on small business. In particular, it recommended that legislators should be obliged to consider the impact on the small business sector of every new piece of legislation. It suggested that key Government departments should have "user groups" comprising of entrepreneurs and managers of small businesses. The Task Force also suggested that there be a Small Business Act that would give effect to many of the recommendation in their Report.

Forfás

In addition, Forfás has played an important role in contributing to the development of a knowledge-based economy, by producing seminal publications, such as *Broadband Investment in Ireland* (March 1998), *Telecommunications: A Key Contributor in Competitiveness and Electronic Commerce* (November 1998) and the *Report on E-Commerce: The Policy Requirement* (July 1999).

The recommendations of these publications impact all Irish businesses. For example, the recommendation of the *Report on E-Commerce* included:

- Assist Irish-owned firms to move up the value chain from bespoke software to world class niches and other products (Enterprise Ireland and Shannon Development)

- Promote Ireland as the premier EU location from which to distribute content products digitally

- Encourage major music, media and information publishers to centralise digital distribution in Ireland and to undertake value added activities, such as media asset management and royalty collection and remittance (IDA Ireland)

- Encourage Irish-owned electronics SMEs to develop e-commerce capabilities in their supplier chains using Internet solutions (Enterprise Ireland and Shannon Development)

- Encourage universities and institutions from other countries to locate their distance learning centres in Ireland (IDA Ireland).

Government and Other Agencies Supporting Enterprise

There are a large number of State agencies that support new and small businesses in Ireland. Most of these agencies provide financial support in the form of grants or cheap loans. Increasingly, agencies are emphasising non-financial advice, such as mentoring support, access to networks, and business planning advice.

In addition to these, there are many smaller, specialist and locally-based State and private sector agencies.

For a comprehensive listing of agencies, see the "Assistance" section of www.startingabusinessinireland.com.

CONCLUSION

The economic, social, cultural, state and regional factors that influence the level of entrepreneurship in a economy were discussed in this chapter. These factors are all important in determining the level and type of entrepreneurship. It is apparent that economic factors are important in accounting for the overall level of entrepreneurial activity in an economy. However, accounting for the level of entrepreneurship will not explain the level of economic growth achieved. Social and culture factors explain the type of person that chooses to act entrepreneurially. Reports on industrial policy have suggested ways in which an enterprise culture could be developed in Ireland and how the State can best support and encourage entrepreneurship.

QUESTIONS

1. Outline a model of the factors that influence entrepreneurial activity. Apply this model to Ireland.

2. How do economic factors influence the level of entrepreneurship?

3. Discuss how the State influences the level of enterprise in an economy?

4. Discuss whether Ireland has an "enterprise culture". What factors may have mitigated against the emergence of entrepreneurship in Ireland?

5. Chose one State agency involved in supporting new or small businesses. Write a report on the supports it offers.

6. Write a report for the Government outlining the policies you believe should be implemented to increase the level of enterprise in Ireland.

REFERENCES

Task Force on Small Business (1994): (Seamus Brennan, Chairman), Dublin: Stationery Office.

Industrial Policy Review Group (1991): *A Time For Change: Industrial Policy for the 1990s*, Report of the Industrial Policy Review Group, (J. Culliton, Chairperson), Dublin: Stationary Office.

12

COMMUNITY ENTERPRISE

INTRODUCTION[14]

The Irish Government and the European Union have recognised that there are urban and rural areas that must be specifically targeted if they are to participate fully in economic development. In this chapter, the factors that have created the need for a local and community-based approach to encouraging enterprise are considered. This new approach to planning is based on involving all the "social partners" in the development of structures that support local communities. An integrated development approach to economic development seeks to bring together the social partners, the community, the voluntary sector and the statutory agencies in a process of defining economic and social needs and of planning and implementing activities. The policy responses of the European Union are discussed.

THE NEED FOR AN INTEGRATED APPROACH

Decline in Rural Areas

Rural areas account for more than 80 percent of the territory of the European Union but are home to only 15 percent of its population. These regions are becoming increasingly diverse in terms of population, employment patterns and the structure of economic activity. In the most remote regions, where rural traditions have remained strongest, the population is in steady decline and the economic and social fabric is becoming increasingly "fragile". Ireland's peripheral rural areas suffer from many disparities.

These disparities include:

- **Remote Location**: Many of these areas are both remote in terms of geography and economics.

---

[14] This chapter was contributed by Dr. Shelia Flanagan, Department of Hospitality Management and Tourism, Dublin Institute of Technology.

- **Demographics**: These areas are suffering from population decline. Those that are remaining in rural areas are ageing.

- **Decline in Agricultural**: There is a general downward trend in agricultural activities world-wide. This is resulting in rural unemployment. Agriculture has become a minority activity in Europe, accounting for only about six percent of employment in 1991 compared with over 13 percent in 1970.

- **World Economics**: The GATT Agreements, continued EU economic convergence and the increased co-operation with emerging Central Europe all present new challenges to rural communities.

- **Poor Infrastructure**: These areas suffer from a lack of infrastructure that is essential for economic development.

- **Withdrawal of Service**: Many community services have been discontinued in rural areas. This increases the isolation of these areas.

- **Poor Skills**: There tends to be an inadequate skills base in rural areas.

- **Lack of Industry Locally**: Businesses in rural areas tend to be low technology enterprises. Many rural areas are over dependent on large employers.

- **Remoteness**: Remoteness from innovation and information centres makes development more difficult.

Of particular significance to rural communities is the continued mismatch between supply and demand of agricultural produce. This has prompted a reform of the Common Agricultural Policy (CAP). The future of rural society cannot depend on agriculture alone but rather it depends on rural development measures that embrace the diversification of rural enterprise, promotion of agribusiness and the development of small and medium sized enterprises.

Decline in Urban Areas

In an urban context, central Government have been motivated into action by the recognition that economic growth by itself will not improve the living conditions and prospects of the most vulnerable groups in Irish society. Of particular importance in this regard are the socially excluded, people who are long-term unemployed and those at risk of becoming long-term unemployed. Disadvantaged urban areas are identified by above average levels of unemployment, long-term unemployment, high rates of early school-leavers, economic dependency, lone parent families, temporary housing, a low level of participation in education, and an overall widening of the gap between the rich and the poor. The consequences of unemployment and poverty are manifested in social breakdown, crime, and environmental decay. Of the 35 designated disadvantaged areas in Ireland, 20 are in urban areas, with two-thirds of these located within the Dublin region. The focus of attention of Government policies in urban areas has primarily been on job placement, training for industrial employment and for enterprise creation, the tackling of social problems associated with disadvantaged areas, and overall urban regeneration.

Figure 12.1: The Finglas Partnership

The Finglas Partnership is one of the Area-based Partnership Companies established under the National Programme for Economic and Social Progress (PESP). The Partnership has representatives from the local community and from all of the "social partners", namely the Government, the trade unions and the private sector. The board consists of six community directors, six State agency directors and six social partners. The Partnership has established working groups in the areas of training and education; business development and job creation; public relations; and effective partnership.

The Finglas Partnership has produced an Area Action Plan setting out a range of strategies aimed at tackling long-term unemployment (at one point, as high as 25%). The plan is the result of many meetings between the Partnership and local community groups, employers, social partners, the Department of the Taoiseach, the IDA and Enterprise Ireland, FÁS, the VEC, Dublin Corporation, the Department of Social, Community and Family Affairs, the Enterprise Trust, CERT and the Eastern Health Board.

The key objectives of the Finglas Partnership are:

- *To generate new jobs in Finglas*
- *To support existing companies in their pursuit of growth*
- *To promote Finglas as a desirable business location*
- *To increase the number of education and training programmes for unemployed people in Finglas*
- *To assist and fund community regeneration.*

Factors Triggering Local Enterprise Initiatives
This background of urban and rural deprivation, the ineffectiveness of mainstream policies and programmes, and the need to stimulate enterprise has resulted in the emergence of many local development initiatives, designed and promoted by local communities to address their own needs and to focus national policies and programmes. This acceleration of local enterprise initiatives has been triggered by several factors:

- **Unemployment**: The growing inability of the State to deal with unemployment. Government policies and initiatives developed by central Government have proved too inflexible to cope with local conditions. They have failed to create a local "enterprise culture".

- **Economic Restructuring and Globalisation**: Many regions have suffered the effects of international economic restructuring. This has resulted in unemployment, social discontent and an increased interest in the possibilities of local mobilisation. This often happens as communities initially try to resist the effects of economic restructuring.

- **Centralisation of Policy-making**: Policy-making has become more centralised at a national and at a European level. This has increased the demand for local autonomy and the devolution of authority. It has been recognised that social partnership at the national level, that is the Government acting with national trade unions and other agencies, cannot guarantee the extension of the benefits of economic prosperity to the long-term unemployed and other groups suffering from economic distress.

- **Complex Problems needing Integrated Solutions**: There has been a realisation that the problems of under-development are multi-faceted and cannot be reduced to a single cause, nor solved by a single solution. More effective solutions require closer working relationships among groups with complementary interests. These solutions must be based on negotiated forms of planning, with structures that involve some form of co-operation.

- **Failure of the "Private Sector"**: The focus of the "private sector" is such that it has failed to become involved in many community-based projects.

INTEGRATED POLICY SOLUTIONS

In recent years, developments in both EU and Irish Policy have given rise to a range of programmes directly and indirectly relevant to enterprise development. Public intervention in the promotion of local development activity is a relatively recent phenomenon in Ireland. Most of these initiatives have adopted a "top-down" approach. The dominant characterisation of the "top down" approach is that the ends, such as number of jobs created, are emphasised at the expense of the means. The alternative "bottom up" model focuses on the processes that lead to the establishment of a climate of entrepreneurship at the local level. This model seeks to promote the "know-how" of development at a local level and enable local communities to create their own sustainable jobs. Under this model, the emphasis is switched from support for centrally-selected projects to funding for, and investment in, the development of the knowledge, the skills and the entrepreneurial activities of the local population.

All of this has relevance in an Irish urban and rural context. Through the application for Structural Funds, Ireland was offered a new way of approaching economic development. These funds encouraged actions designed to improve and develop alternative enterprises at county and sub-county levels. The European Union "Local Development Programme"[15] expands on the integrated approach to local development. New structures have been developed to co-ordinate local development activities. Area Development Management (ADM) is responsible for the EU initiatives for integrated development in designated disadvantaged areas. The Department of Enterprise, Trade and Employment and the Department of Environment and Local Government are responsible for EU initiatives on local enterprise and urban and village renewal respectively.

The integrated local approach to economic development has received commitment and endorsement from the Irish Government, the Economic & Social Research Institute and the EU. EU policy is that State input needs to be balanced by a stronger "bottom-up" approach to development. However, international experience has shown that local enterprise cannot thrive in a policy vacuum and that it needs judicious "top-down" support from Government and State agencies.

The framework within which local economic development and, specifically, local enterprise creation will take place is based on Area Partnership Companies, LEADER Network companies, Integrated

---

[15] Operational Programme for Local Urban and Rural Development, 1994–1999.

Resource Development (IRD) companies and a growing list of enterprise companies. The Government's local development strategy is to support the evolution of a network of such companies and to establish a new support system of County Enterprise Boards.

Area Partnerships
In its report, *A Strategy for the Nineties*, the National Economic and Social Council recommended an area-based response to social welfare issues and problems. The Programme for Economic and Social Progress (PESP), negotiated between the Government and the social partners, provided for the setting up of Area Partnership Companies in both urban and rural areas to tackle unemployment.

The aim of the Partnership Companies is to ensure that local people are the driving force behind a coherent and integrated approach to the economic, social and cultural development and revitalisation of their community. The Partnership Companies involve community leaders with State agencies, local employers, trade unions and farming body representatives. The decision to pursue local development through an Area Partnership approach grew out of a realisation that economic growth in Ireland had failed to adequately target those who were particularly vulnerable and at the margins of society.

In 1991, 12 regions were selected for Area Partnership Companies. These were Ballymun, Coolock/Darndale, Cork North City, Dublin Inner City, Dundalk, Finglas, Limerick City, North Mayo, South West Kerry, South West Waterford, Tallaght, and West Waterford. In 1994, the Area Partnership Companies were progressively extended nation-wide and their number increased to 38. To date, 1,800 enterprises have been assisted by the Partnerships and almost 1,600 individuals have received training or education in enterprise-related skills.

Figure 12.2: Kiltimagh IRD Development Initiative

Kiltimagh is situated in the centre of County Mayo and serves an area that covers a population of 2,000. This figure has fallen by 14% in the most recent inter-censal period. A survey carried out in 1990 showed that the town had suffered from emigration, a decline in businesses and an ageing population. A group of community activists considered the establishment of a "third sector" company (Kiltimagh Integrated Resource Development) thus adopting the OECD model of development

A key decision taken by IRD Kiltimagh was to appoint a full time manager to help develop, market and encourage small enterprise development. The development focus was on tourism and natural resources. Funding was provided mainly from community sources with 2,000 people contributing €2.54 per week each, matched by employer bodies (€264,100 p.a.) and a three-year grant from Mayo County Development Team (€12,697). IRD Kiltimagh had as its primary objective "the development of the economic potential of Kiltimagh and its environs to the fullest, and in way that would benefit the whole community." This community spirit meant that in 1991 that they were outright winners of the ESB Community Enterprise Awards Scheme.

An cultural/artistic development programme encompassed sculpture, community arts, theatre, an artists' retreat and a cultural centre. The company developed other funding linkages with statutory and local agencies and thus established a firm network through the region, becoming one of the constituents of the Western Rural Development Company Limited, which administrated grant aid through the Leader Programme (1992–1994). IRD Kiltimagh is also linked to the Area Based Partnership (PESP Company).

In planning for the 1995–1999 period, the company engaged the services of a professional facilitator to consult with the community and various agencies. As a result, working groups were established to address and advance project development, including:

- Continued development of small enterprises through home-producers groups in food, hand-crafts and aesthetic art

- Development of services in support of the existing rural tourism programmes including seed capital, family farm programmes, telecottage services, tourism marketing, village enhancement and community arts.

The LEADER Programme[16]

LEADER is a European Initiative for rural development, designed to find innovative solutions to local problems by availing of local organisational capacity and expertise. LEADER enables people to have an input into the development of their own areas by devising strategies that will create employment and wealth. The key activities funded under the Programme include technical support for rural development, vocational training, employment grants, rural tourism, marketing activities, small firms, craft enterprises, agriculture, forestry and fisheries, and the preservation of the environment and of living conditions. In evaluating projects for aid, emphasis is placed on the promoter's background and expertise, the viability of the project, the innovative nature of the project, the market for the product, the potential for job creation, and the benefits to the local area. In addition, new enterprises should not displace existing enterprises.

In Ireland, the LEADER I programme was administered by 16 local action groups, in areas selected on the basis of business plans submitted to the EU Commission via the Department of Agriculture, Food and Forestry. Each company was constituted as a legal entity and some €44 million in public funding was provided to the groups over the period 1991–1994. About 44 percent of the projects funded under LEADER I were in rural tourism.

LEADER II (1996–1999) was a nation-wide programme and was administered locally by selected rural development organisations. It has now come to an end. Its replacement, LEADER+, has an allocation of €2,020 million in the period 2000-2006. LEADER+ is aimed at encouraging and supporting high quality and ambitious integrated strategies for local rural development, putting a strong emphasis on co-operation and networking between rural areas.

County Enterprise Boards

Thirty-six County Enterprise Boards have been established covering county and urban local authority areas. The composition of the boards reflects a balance of political, government, business, farming, trade unions and community interests. Specialist Evaluation Committees comprising persons with banking and accounting experience assist each board in assessing the quality, local relevance and cost-effectiveness of project proposals. County Enterprise Boards will not

---

[16] *Liaison Entr' Actions de developpement de l'economie Rurale* (Links between actions for the development of the rural economy.

normally consider proposals involving grant support in excess of €63,486. The designated task of a County Enterprise Boards is to develop pro-active strategies to tap the employment opportunities of the locality. This involves:

- Developing enterprise action plans covering all business sectors in their area
- Identifying and developing local resources
- The creation of a local enterprise culture
- The creation of enterprises through support for local groups
- Providing grant support to individuals and community groups to prepare business plans
- Providing grant support to individuals and community groups to assist viable enterprise projects
- The provision of employment grants.

Support Agencies

Apart from the role of the County Enterprise Board structure in harnessing financial support for local enterprise, the prime channels for providing direct external assistance are Area Development Management (ADM) and the Foundation for Investing in Communities (formerly the Enterprise Trust).

- **Area Development Management (ADM)**: ADM administers the EU Global Grant for Local Development. This amounted to 10 million ECU for the period up to December 1993. This money was provided mainly to the Area Partnership Companies and other community groups. In accordance with EU matching fund requirements, ADM expects 25% of funding to come from non-EU sources. These may include other grants, exchequer funds, and local fund-raising. ADM's priorities are:
  ◊ The provision of direct funding to community groups to enable them to prepare and implement plans for economic and social development;
  ◊ The provision of a "bridging mechanism" to encourage groups to plan an agenda for action in advance of the next round of EU Structural Funds.
- **Foundation for Investing in Communities**: The Foundation for Investing in the Communities incorporates the Enterprise Trust, which was the response of Irish employers to the problem of long-term unemployment. Its objectives are to create sustainable

businesses and to ensure that the unemployed benefit as a result. The Foundation has built an employer network nationally to support local initiatives and to minimise the dangers of job displacement. It therefore encourages businesses to concentrate on exports, import substitution and tourism. It is committed to funding the enterprise activities of approved Area Partnership Programmes and to supporting local enterprise companies that commit themselves to agreed local matching fund arrangements.

CONCLUSION

Local development can act as a catalyst for economic and social development. Local development is not a new concept in Ireland. Over the years, there have been many initiatives by the State to encourage local development. However, the emphasis that the European Union has placed on local development has meant that it has become a key policy instrument for economic development. Underlying the evolution of integrated development initiatives in Ireland are processes of change within the Ireland and the EU. However, more recently, Partnerships have become involved in such areas as working with refugees and asylum-seekers, which were not part of their core objectives at inception.

QUESTIONS

1. What factors have created the need for an integrated approach to rural and urban development?
2. Describe two initiatives that support an integrated and community approach to economic development.
3. Find out what services and incentives are available from your local County Enterprise Board? What contribution has the County Enterprise Board made to economic development in your region?

REFERENCES

Barry, T. (1995): *EU Rural Development Policy and Its Impact on Local Government in Ireland*, Limerick County Enterprise Board, Limerick.

Government of Ireland (1994): *Operational Programme: Local Urban and Rural Development, 1994–1999*, Dublin.

Government of Ireland (1994): *National Development Plan, 1994–1999*, Dublin.

Higgins, J. (1996): *The Kiltimagh Renewal — Best Practice in Community Enterprise*, Cork: Oak Tree Press.

E-COMMERCE GLOSSARY

Archie: A file locating system whereby a user can search for a particular file available through anonymous FTP, provided they know the filename, and can access one of many Archie servers from a listing of filenames. Archie will also provide information on where the particular files are located.

Auto-responders: A feature of e-mail that automatically sends an electronic message to a user who submits a request. From a business perspective this allows for the unattended provision of product descriptions and company information.

Bulletin Boards: Electronic BBS allow dial-up access to a remote computer, giving users access to information and postings of interest to them on a specific topic. These are operated by computer hobbyists and so the topics are broad. Businesses can provide customers with dial-up authorisation passwords for bulletin boards posting company or product information.

Electronic Mail: E-mail allows the user to electronically send and receive messages. Within a closed network such as a Local Area Network (LAN), messages can only be sent to and received from other users on the LAN. With Internet, e-mail the user can communicate electronically with any of the millions of Internet users. Each e-mail user, whether on a local network or on the Internet, has an unique e-mail address. If connected to the Internet the address will include the Internet connection node identifier such as the organisation's domain name, JSmith@system.company.com. E-mail allows a single user to send a message to one or many recipients, to forward messages and to receive messages from one or many senders. Internet e-mail allows for the creation of discussion groups, mailing lists and auto-responders, bringing businesses close to their constituents.

File Transfer Protocol: With FTP and the appropriate access authority, a user can transfer a computer file (text, audio or video) in its original form from a remote system to their own, or *vice versa*. It is especially useful to businesses with significant electronic communication requirements.

Gopher: A menu listing of Internet items maintained by site system administrators. Menus may link the user to a text file, to an Archie server or even to another Gopher menu. Due to the navigation sophistication and simplicity of use, Gopher menus have been used by businesses to establish Gopher-based storefronts.

Internet Relay Chat (IRC): This feature allows for the real-time discussion between Internet users. It is like a CB radio in both style and content.

Intranets: Intranets are private Nets or "intranets" that use the infrastructure and standards of the Internet and the WWW but are cordoned off from the public Internet through software programs known as "fire walls". This allows the user to use the WWW, but unauthorised users cannot access some areas of a site. Therefore the businesses need for paper and physical storage space can be reduced. The same electronic information can be stored on computer and viewed by appropriate employees. In essence this means that all sorts of documents such as internal phone books, procedure manuals, and training materials, can be converted to an electronic format on the WWW and can be constantly updated for minimum cost. By presenting the information in the same format to every computer a business can actually pull together all the computers, software and databases that they may have and put them into a single system that enables employees access any information. The intranets where developed in large businesses but with further developments of intranet based technologies small businesses can avail of the benefits.

Mailing Lists: These lists are a collection of comments and discussions on one particular topic. The list is usually monitored and edited by a moderator, and postings are automatically sent to subscribers' electronic mailboxes on a regular basis. As with News groups, businesses can benefit by monitoring mailing lists of interest to them or about them.

Remote Access Telnet: This application allows users to remotely log into their own or another server, for example a university libraries. As with FTP and Telnet it requires the user to provide an access code identifier.

USENET newsgroups: These newsgroups are Internet accessible bulletin boards on a very broad range of topics. News groups are devoted to specific issues, including technical, recreational and business issues. The participant can simply view the information posted or may post their own comments or responses. Businesses can monitor or participate in newsgroups to obtain information about a topic of interest to them.

Veronica: A database of Gopher menus that allows the user to search for anonymous FTP filenames and to create their own customised Gopher menu. Users are automatically connected when a particular menu item is selected.

WAIS: An acronym for Wide Area Information Servers. WAIS allows for the search of the Internet for a specific topic using everyday language. There are no special requirements and the search is accomplished using some keywords. These tools are operated by Internet search engines such as Altavista, Lycos, Infoseek and like similar search tools provide the user with a menu listing of other Internet resources. The use of the tool is dependent on accurate, easy to locate information, and for businesses its is imperative that there web page address are included in WAIS databases.

World Wide Web (WWW): The WWW is essentially text and images but recent developments mean that sound and video can now be included. Access to the WWW needs software called a browser. For small businesses the information on WWW sites may be of benefit, for example tracking the events in their industry sector on a world-wide basis. The information on WWW sites is usually centred around products, services, pricing, and financial and technical information. Some businesses operating web sites have sections of the site devoted to the company press releases and a section on the history of the business to date. Most web sites with have e-mail addresses of various people in the organisation. A business/individual can use these e-mail links to access more specific information or questions. Some of the best WWW sites have links to sites usually related to the type of business or activity of the firm. In addition most national governments, their agencies and semi-state organisations in addition to the EU, voluntary organisations and marketing co-ops have similar information.

INDEX

OAK TREE PRESS

Oak Tree Press, Ireland's leading business book publisher, has a special focus on micro-enterprise development and is increasingly a developer and publisher of enterprise training and support solutions.

It publishes a range of start-up guides:

- Successful Micro Entrepreneurship: Applying the Rules of Business
- Planning for Success: A Business Plan Workbook for Start-ups
- Starting Your Own Business: A Workbook
- Starting a Business in Ireland

as well as pre-start-up publications:

- Look Before You Leap: A Guide to Self-Employment
- Fire in the Belly: An Exploration of the Entrepreneurial Spirit

and the website, www.startingabusinessinireland.com

It is currently developing a range of growth-focused publications.

In addition, Oak Tree Press has developed SPOTcheck, a web-based (www.spotcheckonline.com) business assessment tool. SPOTcheck:

- Provides a framework against which owner/managers and consultants can make a structured assessment of a business' potential for growth
- Provides a basis for prescribing the appropriate business development interventions for the business
- Tracks progress between SPOTcheck assessments at different times
- Compares the assessment against the averages for similar types of business (benchmarking).

Oak Tree Press has worked extensively in training trainers and as consultants in developing strategic and business plans for both the private and public sector as well as social economy business planning. It has developed a methodology, *Individual Career Path Planning & Self-Employment*, used by the Local Employment Services across Ireland, and under consideration in the UK as a methodology for training business advisers.

Much of Oak Tree Press' enterprise training and support solutions are available for customisation to local situations and needs.

For further information, contact:

Ron Immink or Brian O'Kane
Oak Tree Press
19 Rutland Street, Cork, Ireland
T: + 353 21 431 3855 F: + 353 21 431 3496
E: info@oaktreepress.com